150 best
breakfast
sandwich maker
recipes

Jennifer Williams

Robert
ROSE

For complete cataloguing information, see page 192.

Disclaimer
The recipes in this book have been carefully tested by our kitchen and our tasters. To the best of our knowledge, they are safe and nutritious for ordinary use and users. For those people with food or other allergies, or who have special food requirements or health issues, please read the suggested contents of each recipe carefully and determine whether or not they may create a problem for you. All recipes are used at the risk of the consumer. Consumers should always consult their breakfast sandwich maker manufacturer's manual for recommended procedures and cooking times.

We cannot be responsible for any hazards, loss or damage that may occur as a result of any recipe use.

For those with special needs, allergies, requirements or health problems, in the event of any doubt, please contact your medical adviser prior to the use of any recipe.

Design and production: Martina Hwang/PageWave Graphics Inc.
Editor: Sue Sumeraj
Recipe editor: Jennifer MacKenzie
Proofreader: Sheila Wawanash
Indexer: Gillian Watts
Photographer: Colin Erricson
Associate photographer: Matt Johannsson
Food stylist: Kathryn Robertson
Prop stylist: Charlene Erricson

Cover image: Classic Canadian Bacon and Cheddar Sandwich (page 14)

Chapter opener illustration: Seamless Pop Background © iStockphoto.com/sx70.
Other photographs: Baby Spinach © iStockphoto.com/Kativ; Background with Cucumbers © iStockphoto.com/miolana; Variety of Coloured Bell Peppers © iStockphoto.com/anzeletti; Eggs © iStockphoto.com/zoom-zoom; Bacon Frying on Fry Pan © iStockphoto.com/LauriPatterson; Tomatoes © iStockphoto.com/hdagli; Smoked Salmon © iStockphoto.com/MarkGillow; Olives © iStockphoto.com/kgerakis; Lemons © iStockphoto.com/Dimitris66; Avocado Halves © iStockphoto.com/FotografiaBasica; Close-Up of Red Onion Slices © iStockphoto.com/spaxiax; Cheddar Slices © iStockphoto.com/FotografiaBasica.

The publisher gratefully acknowledges the financial support of our publishing program by the Government of Canada through the Canada Book Fund.

Published by Robert Rose Inc.
120 Eglinton Avenue East, Suite 800, Toronto, Ontario, Canada M4P 1E2
Tel: (416) 322-6552 Fax: (416) 322-6936
www.robertrose.ca

Printed and bound in Canada

5 6 7 8 9 MI 22 21 20 19 18 17 16

Contents

◇◇◇

Introduction

I never intended to write a book of breakfast sandwich recipes. I wasn't a recipe developer or a cookbook author or a food writer of any kind; I was just a mother who, like many other mothers in any given year, was getting my daughter ready to go off to her first year of college. She would be sharing an apartment with other girls and needed to stock her kitchen. As we were packing up her grandmother's old china and glasses, we realized we had overlooked a rather large detail: she had nothing in which to cook her meals. No microwave, no toaster oven, not even a collection of pots and pans.

As a mother, one of the many things you worry about is making sure your children eat filling and nutritious meals. And for a college student, meals need to be as simple and fast as possible; they're simply not going to bother with complicated, time-consuming recipes, healthy or otherwise. So during our excursions to look for kitchen equipment, we were focused on finding tools and appliances that would enable my daughter to prepare nutritious food quickly and easily. On one such outing, we discovered a breakfast sandwich maker, a compact appliance that promised to cook breakfast, one of the most important meals of the day, in just 5 minutes. Sold!

We started testing the appliance by cooking the types of breakfast sandwiches found in fast-food restaurants. But we soon realized there was so much more we could do with this handy little machine. After many wonderful tests (and, truth be told, some downright awful ones), I came up with 35 fast, easy and delicious sandwiches that my daughter could make at college. What I wasn't expecting were the requests from friends for copies of my recipes. As the requests kept coming in, it dawned on me: these sandwiches aren't just a great idea for students; they're perfect for anyone who wants a speedy, tasty and healthy breakfast. It was then that I decided to publish *The Ultimate Breakfast Sandwich* cookbook.

After some great success with this small cookbook, I was contacted by publisher Bob Dees of Robert Rose Inc., who asked if I would be willing to create a book of 150 breakfast sandwich recipes. I jumped at this incredible opportunity, and the result is *150 Best Breakfast Sandwich Maker Recipes*.

This book expands the boundaries of the breakfast sandwich. Sure, you can make a classic breakfast sandwich any time you want — a Classic Canadian Bacon and Cheddar Sandwich (page 14), perhaps, or Bacon and Cream Cheese on a Bagel (page 16) — but you now have many more options at your fingertips when you're looking for some variety. From kid-friendly to gourmet, there's something here for every taste, including gluten-free and vegetarian recipes. Many of these are familiar, traditional sandwiches: a selection of meat, cheese and veggies in between two pieces of bread or on a bun. But who says a sandwich has to be made on bread? Why not pancakes, or waffles, or hash browns, or sausages, or even cake?

Since we're breaking down boundaries, why limit yourself to making breakfast sandwiches for breakfast? Many of the sandwiches in this book will work for lunch too — or even dinner — and there's an entire chapter devoted to dessert and snacks. And don't stop at sandwiches just because that word is in the name of the appliance. With a little bit of ingenuity, you'll find that this clever machine can help you make great burgers, omelets and mini pizzas, too!

The best part? All of these meals can be prepared in very little time, with ingredients you're likely to have on hand in your kitchen.

Happy sandwich making!

Acknowledgments

I cannot even begin to thank the many people who made this book possible without first and foremost giving my heartfelt thanks to my mother. Her endless love and encouragement taught me that you can accomplish anything. Without that, this book would not have been possible. She was a fabulous cook and always made sure we had delicious, healthy meals on the table. I wish she were here now to see this book come to life.

My wonderful daughter, Natalie, has been an enthusiastic supporter and helper as I wrote this book. She inspired the recipes in the first place and has been a tremendous help with recipe ideas, endless taste testing and keeping me laughing when things were getting a little bit crazy. I always love doing things with her, and I respect her opinions.

My amazing friends were so encouraging about this project and shared their time and ideas. My dearest friend, Karla Rabusch, immediately purchased a breakfast sandwich maker and began testing my recipes. Her feedback and support were invaluable. She also shared many ideas for recipe variations — particularly for spicy ingredients, which aren't always on my radar. My friend Kristine Jenstead gave me incredible support and encouragement throughout the process. She is a wonderful chef and shared terrific ingredient ideas. She spent many hours with me and a glass of wine, engaging in endless conversations about this book.

My sincere thanks and appreciation to Bob Dees, my publisher, who trusted me to deliver on this book even though I was a new cookbook author. My editor, Sue Sumeraj, was outstanding to work with. She had tremendous patience with this "newbie." I have learned so much from both Sue and Jennifer MacKenzie, a recipe developer and author, about what makes a great recipe and cookbook.

Many thanks also to Martina Hwang of PageWave Graphics Inc. for the wonderful design, to the photography team at Colin Erricson Photography Inc., who created the beautiful photographs, and to all of the outstanding professionals at Robert Rose Inc., who made this process truly enjoyable and an amazing experience.

Getting Started

About the Breakfast Sandwich Maker

The breakfast sandwich maker is a small electric kitchen appliance that is about 6 inches (15 cm) in diameter and about 6 inches (15 cm) high. This handy little gadget takes up about one-quarter of the space that many kitchen appliances do and will get far more use.

The breakfast sandwich maker has two cooking plates, each with a ring around it, and a cover. The lower cooking plate is where you place the bottom half of the bun or slice of bread and many of the meats, cheeses, fruits and vegetables you are adding to your sandwich. The egg is cooked on the upper cooking plate, covered by the top half of the bun or slice of bread. This cooking plate cooks an egg in 4 to 5 minutes, depending on how you like it.

The breakfast sandwich maker will not cook meats, so any meats you use must be cooked before you add them to the sandwich maker. It will, however, heat meats that have been cooked and frozen, so you do not have to thaw frozen meat before use.

Once the cooking time is up, the upper cooking plate rotates away from the sandwich maker, so when you open it up and lift the rings, you have a perfectly assembled breakfast sandwich that is hot and ready to eat.

It is important to clean the breakfast sandwich maker after each use by washing it in soap and water or wiping it with a damp towel. If you leave oils or leftover ingredients on the cooking surfaces and then reheat them, it will be much harder to remove them the next time you wash the sandwich maker.

Other Handy Equipment

Aside from the sandwich maker, there are just a few other kitchen tools that you will need to make your breakfast sandwiches.

- **Plastic or nylon spatula:** This is used to remove the sandwich from the breakfast sandwich maker. Because the sandwich maker has a nonstick cooking surface, do not touch it with any metal utensils.

- **Cookie cutter or kitchen shears:** To fit nicely into the rings of the breakfast sandwich maker, your bread, buns, rolls or other sandwich "holders" will need to be cut into 4-inch (10 cm) rounds. The easiest tool to use for this purpose is a 4-inch (10 cm) round cookie cutter, but if you don't have one, kitchen shears will also work.
- **Ramekins:** You'll need two ¾-cup (175 mL) ramekins to make a couple of sandwiches in this book that require a mold to form the ingredients. They will also come in handy as small mixing bowls or for whisking an egg.

The Breakfast Sandwich Pantry

The beauty of making your own breakfast sandwiches at home is that you can make them exactly the way you like them, using quality ingredients. You can use fresh or frozen ingredients that you always have on hand in your kitchen, special items that you bought just to try one of these recipes, or even leftovers that you want to use up.

Breads and Buns

If you were asked to name a breakfast sandwich bread, an English muffin might be the first thing that came to mind. English muffins are the perfect size, shape and density for a breakfast sandwich, and many of my recipes do in fact use one. But there are so many other options, from whole wheat and multigrain bread to sourdough and French bread. I like to use a bread that is a little denser, as it will hold up better when packed with ingredients. When you pinch your bread, if it holds that shape and looks something like a paper towel, it probably isn't an ideal choice for your sandwich.

Soft or crusty rolls, brioche buns, baguettes and sandwich buns are, of course, great for sandwiches. When using these types of buns, you may want to scoop out a little bread from the center of the bottom half so that it is less thick, the ingredients fit better inside it, and any liquid ingredients are better contained inside the sandwich. If the top half is too thick to fit well in the sandwich maker, you may want to slice a portion off the top or flatten it a bit with your hand.

Flatbreads, focaccia and bagels hold up particularly well in the breakfast sandwich maker and give your sandwich a unique twist. You can often find mini versions of these breads that will fit perfectly into your sandwich maker. Frozen pancakes and waffles are another fun option.

While each of my recipes specifies a particular type of bread, you can use any type that you prefer or that you have in your kitchen. Whatever bread you use, if it's not already the right size to fit in the breakfast sandwich maker, you will need to cut it into 4-inch (10 cm) rounds.

Eggs

The recipes in this book use large eggs. If you have small, medium or extra-large eggs, you can use them, but you will need to adjust the cooking time accordingly. It is best to store your eggs in the carton they came in and not in the open trays built into your refrigerator, where they can pick up unwanted flavors and odors from other items.

Cheeses

Breakfast sandwiches can be made with just about any type of cheese. Semi-hard, semi-soft, soft, fresh, ripened and blue are some of my favorites for these sandwiches. The key is to pick a cheese that pairs well with the other ingredients. Make sure the cheese is contained inside your sandwich so it doesn't melt all over the inside of your breakfast sandwich maker.

Meat and Fish

Any meat or fish you use in your breakfast sandwich needs to be cooked first. The breakfast sandwich maker will heat up meats and fish, but it will not cook them. You can use deli meats, canned fish, frozen cooked meats, packaged cooked meat or fish, cooked sausages, leftovers — any meat or fish that has been fully cooked, either before or after you purchased it.

Fruits, Vegetables and Herbs

Whether fresh, frozen or canned, just about any fruits or vegetables will add flavor and texture to your sandwich. If using fresh, you'll get the best results by choosing produce that is in season in your area. Not only will the flavor and texture be better, but local in-season fruits and vegetables often cost less.

When adding fresh or dried herbs to your sandwich, remember that a little goes a long way.

Condiments and Toppings

Mayonnaise, butter, mustard and ketchup are standard sandwich spreads, but my recipes also feature marmalades, jams, pizza sauce, pesto, salsa, guacamole, tapenade, spicy peanut sauce, maple syrup, hollandaise sauce, caramel sauce and chocolate sauce, as well as toppings such as roasted nuts, chia seeds and sprouts. Scan the ingredient lists of the recipes that appeal to you to make sure you have everything you need for the sandwiches you want to prepare.

Get Ready, Get Set

You will have the most success with your breakfast sandwiches if you prepare all of the ingredients ahead of time and have them ready to go as soon as the breakfast sandwich maker is preheated. The appliance works quickly, in 5 minutes or less, so if you take too much time to assemble the sandwich, some of the ingredients may get overcooked or may melt too much.

Remember that cooked meats and raw eggs should not sit out at room temperature for more than 30 minutes. (This should not be an issue, as the prep times for most of my recipes are less than 10 minutes, but it's an important reminder!)

Quick Tips for a Great Sandwich

◆ You can use nonstick cooking spray to lightly spray the top or underside of any cooking surface the ingredients are touching, to prevent sticking or overbrowning. This isn't usually necessary, but, for some sandwiches, you may find that it improves the results.

◆ Make sure the ingredients fit easily within the sandwich rings and are not packed in tightly or running over the edges. Use a cookie cutter or kitchen shears to cut all oversize ingredients to the right size and shape.

◆ Do not overstuff ingredients in either layer of the sandwich. The sandwich will cook better and will be easier to handle if you stick to the amounts recommended in the recipes.

◆ When closing the cover of the breakfast sandwich maker, do not press it down on top of the sandwich. Just close it gently and the sandwich will cook perfectly. If you press the cover down, you risk squeezing out the ingredients and ending up with a mess.

◆ Experiment. It only takes 5 minutes to make a breakfast sandwich, but it can take a little experimentation to get the process down just right and the timing perfect for the best results.

Safety Tips

◆ Be careful when raising and lowering the rings and when rotating the cooking plate away from the sandwich maker. Make sure to touch only the handles and/or use a potholder. The sandwich maker gets very hot, including some of the outer edges.

◆ If you are making a sandwich to pack for lunch or a snack later in the day, make sure you have an insulated cooler or can refrigerate your sandwich. It should not be left unrefrigerated for any extended length of time.

Classic Breakfast Sandwiches and Omelets

◇◇◇

Classic Canadian Bacon and Cheddar Sandwich

A classic breakfast sandwich, just like the famous fast-food version, made in the comfort of your home with your choice of quality ingredients.

PREP TIME:
2 MINUTES

COOK TIME:
4 TO 5 MINUTES

Tip

You may know Canadian bacon as back bacon, which is what it is called in many parts of the world. It is actually more similar to ham than to bacon, as it is much leaner and is cut from the loin. This type of bacon is fully cooked. If you want to use peameal bacon (cornmeal-crusted cured pork loin), you will need to cook it before adding it to the sandwich maker.

◆ Preheat breakfast sandwich maker

1	English muffin, split in half	1
1	slice Cheddar cheese	1
1	slice Canadian bacon	1
	Nonstick cooking spray	
1	large egg	1
Pinch	freshly ground black pepper (optional)	Pinch
Pinch	salt (optional)	Pinch

1. Place one English muffin half, split side up, in bottom ring of sandwich maker. Top with cheese and bacon.

2. Lower the cooking plate and top ring. Lightly spray the plate with cooking spray, then crack the egg into the ring. Pierce top of egg yolk with a toothpick or plastic fork. Season with salt and pepper (if using). Place the other muffin half, split side down, on top of the egg.

3. Gently close the cover and cook for 4 to 5 minutes or until egg is cooked to your liking. Rotate cooking plate away from sandwich maker and lift rings. Use a plastic or nylon spatula to remove the sandwich. Serve immediately.

Variation

Use 2 egg whites, instead of the whole egg, if you are looking to reduce your cholesterol intake. The yolk contains most of the fat and cholesterol, but keep in mind that it also supplies most of the nutrients, such as vitamins A and D, phosphorus, folate and calcium.

Bacon, Tomato and Swiss Sandwich

Almost like a BLT for breakfast, but with an added punch of protein that will give your body a boost to start the day.

| PREP TIME: |
| **2 MINUTES** |

| COOK TIME: |
| **4 TO 5 MINUTES** |

Tips

Cook up a package of bacon ahead of time and store in your refrigerator to use for quick breakfast sandwiches. Seal the cooked bacon tightly in an airtight container or tin foil for up to 1 week.

If you would like to use thick-cut bacon, use 2 slices instead of 3.

◆ Preheat breakfast sandwich maker

1 tbsp	mayonnaise	15 mL
1	English muffin, split in half	1
1	slice tomato	1
1	slice Swiss cheese	1
3	slices bacon, cooked crisp	3
	Nonstick cooking spray	
1	large egg	1

1. Spread mayonnaise on split sides of English muffin. Place one muffin half, split side up, in bottom ring of sandwich maker. Top with tomato and cheese. Break bacon into pieces that fit in the ring and add on top of the cheese.

2. Lower the cooking plate and top ring. Lightly spray the plate with cooking spray, then crack the egg into the ring. Pierce top of egg yolk with a toothpick or plastic fork. Place the other muffin half, split side down, on top of the egg.

3. Gently close the cover and cook for 4 to 5 minutes or until egg is cooked to your liking. Rotate cooking plate away from sandwich maker and lift rings. Use a plastic or nylon spatula to remove the sandwich. Serve immediately.

Variations

Add lettuce to your sandwich after removing it from the sandwich maker, to make it taste even more like a classic BLT.

Use 2 slices of whole wheat bread in place of the English muffin. Cut each slice into a round that fits the sandwich maker rings.

Bacon and Cream Cheese on a Bagel

So easy and filling for an on-the-go breakfast. The flavor variations are endless: just choose different flavors of cream cheese and different types of bagels.

PREP TIME:
3 MINUTES

COOK TIME:
4 TO 5 MINUTES

Tips

You may have to trim your bagel halves slightly around the edges to fit properly into the sandwich maker. Kitchen scissors work best for this task.

Thin bagels are not only easier to eat in a sandwich, but also lower in calories.

If you can find it, you can use spreadable cream cheese with chives instead of adding fresh chives.

♦ Preheat breakfast sandwich maker

2 tbsp	spreadable cream cheese	30 mL
1	small thin bagel, split in half	1
3	slices bacon, cooked crisp	3
	Nonstick cooking spray	
1	large egg	1
2 tsp	chopped fresh chives (optional)	10 mL

1. Spread cream cheese on split sides of bagel. Place one bagel half, spread side up, in bottom ring of sandwich maker. Break bacon into pieces that fit in the ring and place on top of the bagel.

2. Lower the cooking plate and top ring. Lightly spray the plate with cooking spray, then crack the egg into the ring. Pierce top of egg yolk with a toothpick or plastic fork. Sprinkle with chives (if using). Place the other bagel half, spread side down, on top of the egg.

3. Gently close the cover and cook for 4 to 5 minutes or until egg is cooked to your liking. Rotate cooking plate away from sandwich maker and lift rings. Use a plastic or nylon spatula to remove the sandwich. Serve immediately.

Variations

Try one of the many varieties of flavored spreadable cream cheese, such as pineapple, green olive or roasted pepper.

Bacon and Cheese on a Golden Biscuit

A warm, flaky, buttery biscuit makes this sandwich pure comfort food. Breakfast doesn't get much easier.

PREP TIME:
1 MINUTE

COOK TIME:
4 TO 5 MINUTES

Tip

To make this sandwich a real down-home treat, serve with a side of warm gravy for dipping.

• Preheat breakfast sandwich maker

1	flaky buttermilk biscuit, split in half	1
1	slice Monterey Jack cheese	1
3	slices bacon, cooked crisp	3
	Nonstick cooking spray	
1	large egg	1

1. Place one biscuit half, split side up, in bottom ring of sandwich maker. Top with cheese. Break bacon into pieces that fit in the ring and place on top of the cheese.

2. Lower the cooking plate and top ring. Lightly spray the plate with cooking spray, then crack the egg into the ring. Pierce top of egg yolk with a toothpick or plastic fork. Place the other biscuit half, split side down, on top of the egg.

3. Gently close the cover and cook for 4 to 5 minutes or until egg is cooked to your liking. Rotate cooking plate away from sandwich maker and lift rings. Use a plastic or nylon spatula to remove the sandwich. Serve immediately.

Variations

Sprinkle a little Worcestershire sauce on the egg (or in the gravy) to add some extra punch.

Substitute 2 oz (60 g) chipped beef for the cooked bacon.

Waffle and Bacon Sandwich

Waffles, bacon and eggs are a breakfast tradition. Here, they come together in a fast and easy sandwich.

PREP TIME:
1 MINUTE

COOK TIME:
4 TO 5 MINUTES

Tip

Kids love to fill the little holes of the waffle with table syrup. They can even fill the holes in the bottom waffle before you place it in the sandwich maker.

♦ Preheat breakfast sandwich maker

2	frozen round waffles	2
1	slice Monterey Jack cheese	1
3	slices bacon, cooked crisp	3
	Nonstick cooking spray	
1	large egg	1
	Table syrup (optional)	

1. Place a waffle in bottom ring of sandwich maker. Top with cheese. Break bacon into pieces that fit in the ring and place on top of the cheese.

2. Lower the cooking plate and top ring. Lightly spray the plate with cooking spray, then crack the egg into the ring. Pierce top of egg yolk with a toothpick or plastic fork. Place the other waffle on top of the egg.

3. Gently close the cover and cook for 4 to 5 minutes or until egg is cooked to your liking. Rotate cooking plate away from sandwich maker and lift rings. Use a plastic or nylon spatula to remove the sandwich. Serve immediately, drizzled with syrup if desired.

Variation

Use pepper Jack cheese instead of Monterey Jack, for a spicier kick to your morning.

Maple Sausage and Egg on Waffles

Pork sausage flavored with maple syrup adds just the right amount of sweetness to this waffle sandwich.

PREP TIME:
1 MINUTE

COOK TIME:
4 TO 5 MINUTES

Tips

You can use square or triangular waffles if you cut them into circles to fit the sandwich maker. Use a round cookie cutter or kitchen shears to cut your waffles.

For a crispier sandwich, lightly toast the waffles ahead of time.

♦ Preheat breakfast sandwich maker

2	frozen round waffles	2
1	frozen cooked maple-flavored pork sausage patty	1
	Nonstick cooking spray	
1	large egg	1
	Pure maple syrup (optional)	

1. Place a waffle in bottom ring of sandwich maker. Top with sausage.

2. Lower the cooking plate and top ring. Lightly spray the plate with cooking spray, then crack the egg into the ring. Pierce top of egg yolk with a toothpick or plastic fork. Place the other waffle on top of the egg.

3. Gently close the cover and cook for 4 to 5 minutes or until egg is cooked to your liking. Rotate cooking plate away from sandwich maker and lift rings. Use a plastic or nylon spatula to remove the sandwich. Serve immediately, drizzled with syrup if desired.

Variation

For a leaner sandwich, use a turkey sausage patty. Turkey sausage is usually about 65% leaner than pork sausage.

Pancake and Sausage Sandwich

Here, many of the traditional breakfast favorites are combined in one quick and easy sandwich.

PREP TIME:
1 MINUTE

COOK TIME:
4 TO 5 MINUTES

Tips

Whenever you make pancakes, make a few extra and freeze them to use in breakfast sandwiches. Or use store-bought frozen pancakes. The pancakes do not need to be thawed before they are placed in the sandwich maker.

Look for frozen sausage patties in the freezer section of the grocery store. Choose regular or flavored sausage patties to suit your taste.

◆ Preheat breakfast sandwich maker

2	frozen pancakes	2
1	slice Cheddar cheese	1
1	frozen cooked pork sausage patty	1
	Nonstick cooking spray	
1	large egg	1

1. Place a pancake in bottom ring of sandwich maker. Top with cheese and sausage.

2. Lower the cooking plate and top ring. Lightly spray the plate with cooking spray, then crack the egg into the ring. Pierce top of egg yolk with a toothpick or plastic fork. Place the other pancake on top of the egg.

3. Gently close the cover and cook for 4 to 5 minutes or until egg is cooked to your liking. Rotate cooking plate away from sandwich maker and lift rings. Use a plastic or nylon spatula to remove the sandwich. Serve immediately.

Sausage and Egg on Hash Browns

This hearty combination surely won't leave you feeling hungry — and it's a great antidote to help you recover from a late night out.

PREP TIME:
5 MINUTES

COOK TIME:
4 TO 5 MINUTES

Tips

If you don't have round hash brown patties, cut the frozen hash browns into 4-inch (10 cm) rounds using a cookie cutter or the metal ring of a wide-mouth canning jar.

Before assembling the sandwich, cook the hash brown patties in the microwave according to the package directions. The patties will get brown and crispy in the sandwich maker.

♦ Preheat breakfast sandwich maker

2	frozen round hash brown patties, cooked (see tips, at left)	2
1	slice sharp (old) Cheddar cheese	1
1	frozen cooked pork sausage patty	1
	Nonstick cooking spray	
1	large egg	1

1. Place a cooked hash brown in bottom ring of sandwich maker. Top with cheese and sausage.

2. Lower the cooking plate and top ring. Lightly spray the plate with cooking spray, then crack the egg into the ring. Pierce top of egg yolk with a toothpick or plastic fork. Place the other hash brown patty on top of the egg.

3. Gently close the cover (do not push it down onto the hash brown) and cook for 4 to 5 minutes or until egg is cooked to your liking. Rotate cooking plate away from sandwich maker and lift rings. Use a plastic or nylon spatula to remove the sandwich. Serve immediately.

Sausage and Applesauce on Cinnamon Bread

With its mix of cinnamon, apple and cream cheese flavors, this sandwich almost tastes like warm apple pie.

PREP TIME:
2 MINUTES

COOK TIME:
4 TO 5 MINUTES

Tip

Use a round cookie cutter, the metal ring of a wide-mouth canning jar or kitchen shears to cut your cinnamon bread into 4-inch (10 cm) rounds.

◆ Preheat breakfast sandwich maker

1 tbsp	cream cheese, softened	15 mL
2	slices cinnamon bread, cut into 4-inch (10 cm) rounds	2
1 tbsp	applesauce	15 mL
1	frozen cooked pork sausage patty	1
	Nonstick cooking spray	
1	large egg	1

1. Spread cream cheese on one side of each bread slice. Place one slice, spread side up, in bottom ring of sandwich maker. Spread applesauce on top. Top with sausage.

2. Lower the cooking plate and top ring. Lightly spray the plate with cooking spray, then crack the egg into the ring. Pierce top of egg yolk with a toothpick or plastic fork. Place the other bread slice, spread side down, on top of the egg.

3. Gently close the cover and cook for 4 to 5 minutes or until egg is cooked to your liking. Rotate cooking plate away from sandwich maker and lift rings. Use a plastic or nylon spatula to remove the sandwich. Serve immediately.

Variations

Cinnamon raisin bread or cinnamon raisin English muffins work equally well in this sandwich.

Substitute 1 tbsp (15 mL) apple butter for the applesauce. Apple butter, a preserve, has a much longer shelf life than applesauce and can be used on many sandwiches and in other recipes.

Ham and Apple on Pancakes

Adding apple slices to a breakfast sandwich, and eating the rest of the apple on the side, is an easy and tasty way to get in one of the recommended daily servings of fruit.

PREP TIME:
2 MINUTES

COOK TIME:
4 TO 5 MINUTES

Tip

I like to use green apples, such as Granny Smith, in this recipe for their added tartness, but any type of apple you have on hand will work just fine.

◆ Preheat breakfast sandwich maker

2	frozen pancakes	2
1	slice Colby cheese	1
2 to 3	slices deli ham	2 to 3
3	slices apple	3
	Nonstick cooking spray	
1	large egg	1

1. Place a pancake in bottom ring of sandwich maker. Top with cheese, ham and apple.

2. Lower the cooking plate and top ring. Lightly spray the plate with cooking spray, then crack the egg into the ring. Pierce top of egg yolk with a toothpick or plastic fork. Place the other pancake on top of the egg.

3. Gently close the cover and cook for 4 to 5 minutes or until egg is cooked to your liking. Rotate cooking plate away from sandwich maker and lift rings. Use a plastic or nylon spatula to remove the sandwich. Serve immediately.

Variations

For a leaner sandwich, use sliced deli turkey in place of the ham.

Replace the Colby cheese with Gouda, which will add a slightly nutty taste to your sandwich.

Ham and Mushroom Omelet

Omelets are a wonderful breakfast treat, but typically take more time than we have on busy mornings. This one is so easy, you may never go back to the traditional cooking method again.

PREP TIME:
5 MINUTES

COOK TIME:
3 TO 4 MINUTES

Tips

When I bake a ham, I make sure to save some leftovers for omelets. I chop or dice the ham and store it in an airtight container in the refrigerator or freezer. Cooked ham can be stored for up to 5 days in the refrigerator or for up to 3 months in the freezer. If using frozen ham, thaw it before adding it to the egg mixture.

You can use fresh or canned mushrooms in this sandwich. If using canned, buy a 4-oz (114 mL) can of mushroom pieces and stems, and drain before dicing.

◆ Preheat breakfast sandwich maker

1	large egg	1
¼ cup	diced cooked ham	60 mL
1 tbsp	diced mushrooms	15 mL
Pinch	salt (optional)	Pinch
Pinch	freshly ground black pepper (optional)	Pinch
	Nonstick cooking spray	

1. In a small bowl, gently whisk egg. Stir in ham and mushrooms. Season with salt and pepper (if using).

2. Lower the cooking plate and both rings of sandwich maker. Lightly spray the cooking plate with cooking spray. Pour the egg mixture into the top ring.

3. Gently close the cover and cook for 3 to 4 minutes or until omelet is cooked to your liking. Rotate cooking plate away from sandwich maker and lift rings. Use a plastic or nylon spatula to remove the omelet. Serve immediately.

Variation

Add 1 tbsp (15 mL) of your favorite shredded cheese with the mushrooms, for creamy, cheesy goodness.

Western Omelet

For a Western omelet, the added ingredients are mixed with the eggs before cooking (instead of being folded into the middle of the partially cooked eggs), so it's the perfect candidate for cooking in a breakfast sandwich maker.

<table>
<tr><td>PREP TIME:
5 MINUTES</td></tr>
</table>

<table>
<tr><td>COOK TIME:
3 TO 4 MINUTES</td></tr>
</table>

Tips

Dice or chop your vegetables in advance and store them in an airtight container in the refrigerator. Once vegetables are cut, they change color or lose firmness more quickly. For best results, use up chopped vegetables within 1 to 3 days.

One of the best things about a Western omelet is that you can mix and match ingredients to your taste. Just keep the total amount of added ingredients to about 6 tbsp (90 mL) or less, so everything will fit in your sandwich maker.

♦ Preheat breakfast sandwich maker

1	large egg	1
1/4 cup	crumbled cooked bacon	60 mL
1 tbsp	diced tomato	15 mL
2 tsp	finely chopped onion	10 mL
2 tsp	finely chopped green bell pepper	10 mL
Pinch	salt (optional)	Pinch
Pinch	freshly ground black pepper (optional)	Pinch
	Nonstick cooking spray	

1. In a small bowl, gently whisk egg. Stir in bacon, tomato, onion and green pepper. Season with salt and pepper (if using).

2. Lower the cooking plate and both rings of sandwich maker. Lightly spray the cooking plate with cooking spray. Pour the egg mixture into the top ring.

3. Gently close the cover and cook for 3 to 4 minutes or until omelet is cooked to your liking. Rotate cooking plate away from sandwich maker and lift rings. Use a plastic or nylon spatula to remove the omelet. Serve immediately.

Variation

Instead of using cooking spray, add 1 1/2 tsp (7 mL) coconut oil to the cooking plate and let it melt slightly before pouring in the egg mixture. Coconut oil adds depth of flavor and is a heart-healthy addition to your diet.

Vegetarian Sandwiches and Omelets

◇◇

Pear and Almond Butter Sandwich

Almond butter is a nice alternative to peanut butter and offers a good dose of protein, while the pear slices contribute to your fruit servings for the day.

PREP TIME:

2 MINUTES

COOK TIME:

4 TO 5 MINUTES

Tips

Do not press the cooking plate and top ring down onto your sandwich. Doing so could cause some of the ingredients to squish out. The sandwich will still cook nicely, and the top bread slice will be lightly toasted.

Eat the remainder of the pear as a side to your morning sandwich or save it in an airtight container for a mid-morning snack.

◆ Preheat breakfast sandwich maker

2 tbsp	almond butter	30 mL
2	slices whole-grain bread, cut into 4-inch (10 cm) rounds	2
½	pear, sliced	½
	Nonstick cooking spray	

1. Spread almond butter on one side of each bread slice. Place one slice, spread side up, in bottom ring of sandwich maker. Top with pear slices and the other bread slice, spread side down.

2. Lightly spray the underside of the cooking plate with cooking spray. Gently lower the cooking plate and top ring. Close the cover and cook for 4 to 5 minutes or until bread is nicely toasted and pears are warm. Rotate cooking plate away from sandwich maker and lift rings. Use a plastic or nylon spatula to remove the sandwich. Serve immediately.

Pear and Gorgonzola on Raisin Bread

The smell of toasting raisin bread is a delightful pick-me-up in the morning. Topping it off with Gorgonzola and pears makes it an even better treat.

PREP TIME:
2 MINUTES

COOK TIME:
4 TO 5 MINUTES

Tip

Bosc pears hold their shape well in a sandwich and have a robust taste that works well with the raisin bread and gorgonzola. Bartlett pears are very juicy and are a nice choice for this recipe if you like your pears softer when heated.

◆ Preheat breakfast sandwich maker

2	slices raisin bread, cut into 4-inch (10 cm) rounds	2
1	slice Gorgonzola cheese	1
¼	pear, sliced	¼
	Nonstick cooking spray	
1	large egg	1

1. Place one bread slice in bottom ring of sandwich maker. Top with cheese and pear.
2. Lower the cooking plate and top ring. Lightly spray the plate with cooking spray, then crack the egg into the ring. Pierce top of egg yolk with a toothpick or plastic fork. Place the other bread slice on top of the egg.
3. Gently close the cover and cook for 4 to 5 minutes or until egg is cooked to your liking. Rotate cooking plate away from sandwich maker and lift rings. Use a plastic or nylon spatula to remove the sandwich. Serve immediately.

Variation

Add some baby spinach leaves before adding the pear for an added nutritional punch.

Avocado, Tomato and Macadamia Nut Sandwich

This sandwich is packed with healthy monounsaturated fats, which are known to reduce belly fat and decrease inflammation. The surprise crunch from the macadamia nuts adds a nice twist.

PREP TIME:
2 MINUTES

COOK TIME:
3 TO 4 MINUTES

Tips

For an open-face sandwich, use only the bottom half of the English muffin.

If your avocado is really nice and ripe, use it as a spread instead of in slices.

◆ Preheat breakfast sandwich maker

1	English muffin, split in half	1
¼	avocado, sliced	¼
1 tbsp	chopped macadamia nuts	15 mL
1	slice tomato	1
	Nonstick cooking spray	
1	large egg white	1

1. Place one English muffin half, split side up, in bottom ring of sandwich maker. Top with avocado, nuts and tomato.

2. Lower the cooking plate and top ring. Lightly spray the plate with cooking spray, then add the egg white. Place the other muffin half, split side down, on top of the egg white.

3. Gently close the cover and cook for 3 to 4 minutes or until egg white is cooked through and no longer translucent. Rotate cooking plate away from sandwich maker and lift rings. Use a plastic or nylon spatula to remove the sandwich. Serve immediately.

Avocado, Tomato and Alfalfa Sprout Sandwich

The creamy rich taste of the avocado, the sweetness of the tomato and the crunch of the alfalfa sprouts makes for a unique and flavorful breakfast combination.

PREP TIME:

2 MINUTES

COOK TIME:

3 TO 4 MINUTES

Tips

For the best flavor, use home-grown or locally grown tomatoes.

Any remaining alfalfa sprouts are a great addition to salads and other types of sandwiches.

◆ Preheat breakfast sandwich maker

1	English muffin, split in half	1
1	slice avocado	1
1	slice tomato	1
	Nonstick cooking spray	
1	large egg white	1
	Alfalfa sprouts	

1. Place one English muffin half, split side up, in bottom ring of sandwich maker. Top with avocado and tomato.

2. Lower the cooking plate and top ring. Lightly spray the plate with cooking spray, then add the egg white. Place alfalfa sprouts on top of the egg white. Place the other muffin half, split side down, on top of the sprouts.

3. Gently close the cover and cook for 3 to 4 minutes or until egg white is cooked through and no longer translucent. Rotate cooking plate away from sandwich maker and lift rings. Use a plastic or nylon spatula to remove the sandwich. Serve immediately.

Variation

In place of the alfalfa sprouts, try other sprouts, such as bean, broccoli, arugula, radish or fenugreek. Each of these will add a slightly different taste, so have fun experimenting.

Egg and Sharp Cheddar on a Golden Biscuit

Enjoy a warm, flaky golden biscuit and a dose of protein without meat, for a healthy morning kick-start.

PREP TIME:
1 MINUTE

COOK TIME:
4 TO 5 MINUTES

Tip

The biscuit used in this recipe is the leavened type, not the cookie or cracker style of biscuit known in some countries.

♦ Preheat breakfast sandwich maker

1	baking powder biscuit, split in half	1
1	slice sharp (old) Cheddar cheese	1
	Nonstick cooking spray	
1	large egg	1
Pinch	salt (optional)	Pinch
Pinch	freshly ground black pepper (optional)	Pinch

1. Place one biscuit half, split side up, in bottom ring of sandwich maker. Top with cheese.

2. Lower the cooking plate and top ring. Lightly spray the plate with cooking spray, then crack the egg into the ring. Pierce top of egg yolk with a toothpick or plastic fork. Season with salt and pepper (if using). Place the other biscuit half, split side down, on top of the egg.

3. Gently close the cover and cook for 4 to 5 minutes or until egg is cooked to your liking. Rotate cooking plate away from sandwich maker and lift rings. Use a plastic or nylon spatula to remove the sandwich. Serve immediately.

Variations

Use 2 egg whites, instead of the whole egg, if you are looking to reduce your cholesterol intake. The yolk contains most of the fat and cholesterol, but keep in mind that it also supplies most of the nutrients, such as vitamins A and D, phosphorus, folate and calcium.

Buttermilk biscuits or scones can be used instead of the baking powder biscuit.

Florentine Sandwich

Simple, elegant and low-calorie, this spinach and egg creation with a light mustard-yogurt spread will delight your taste buds.

PREP TIME:
2 MINUTES

COOK TIME:
4 TO 5 MINUTES

Tips

Any remaining spinach leaves make a great addition to other sandwiches or a delicious salad for lunch.

For an open-face sandwich, leave the top half of the English muffin off.

♦ Preheat breakfast sandwich maker

1 tbsp	plain yogurt	30 mL
½ tsp	Dijon mustard	2 mL
1	English muffin, split in half	1
¼ cup	baby spinach leaves	60 mL
	Nonstick cooking spray	
1	large egg	1
Pinch	salt (optional)	Pinch
Pinch	freshly ground black pepper (optional)	Pinch

1. Spread yogurt and mustard on split side of one English muffin half. Place muffin half, spread side up, in bottom ring of sandwich maker. Top with spinach.

2. Lower the cooking plate and top ring. Lightly spray the plate with cooking spray, then crack the egg into the ring. Pierce top of egg yolk with a toothpick or plastic fork. Season with salt and pepper (if using). Place the other muffin half, split side down, on top of the egg.

3. Gently close the cover and cook for 4 to 5 minutes or until egg is cooked to your liking. Rotate cooking plate away from sandwich maker and lift rings. Use a plastic or nylon spatula to remove the sandwich. Serve immediately.

Variation

Use any variety of mustard you like in place of the Dijon mustard. Good options include coarse, stone-ground and honey mustard. I personally would not use yellow mustard, as it does not add the same extra zing to this sandwich.

Mediterranean Egg White Sandwich

Spinach, sun-dried tomatoes and basil pesto bring a Mediterranean flair to your breakfast table.

Tips

If using pine nuts, choose nuts from a good-quality source. Some people find that pine nuts can give foods a metallic, somewhat bitter taste. However, pine nuts sourced from the U.S., Europe or Turkey do not typically cause this adverse reaction.

I use toasted pine nuts because I like the extra flavor and slight crunch that toasting provides. Untoasted pine nuts will work just as well, but will be softer and have a lighter, more buttery flavor.

♦ Preheat breakfast sandwich maker

1 tbsp	basil pesto	15 mL
1	mini ciabatta roll (about 4 inches/10 cm in diameter), split in half	1
2	oil-packed sun-dried tomatoes, drained and sliced	2
¼ cup	chopped spinach	60 mL
	Nonstick cooking spray	
2	large egg whites	2
1 tsp	toasted pine nuts (optional)	5 mL

1. Spread pesto on split side of one roll half. Place roll half, spread side up, in bottom ring of sandwich maker. Top with sun-dried tomatoes and spinach.

2. Lower the cooking plate and top ring. Lightly spray the plate with cooking spray, then add the egg whites. Sprinkle with pine nuts (if using). Place the other roll half, split side down, on top of the egg whites.

3. Gently close the cover and cook for 4 to 5 minutes or until egg whites are cooked through and no longer translucent. Rotate cooking plate away from sandwich maker and lift rings. Use a plastic or nylon spatula to remove the sandwich. Serve immediately.

Sun-Dried Tomato and Black Olive Sandwich

The sun-drenched flavors in this sandwich make for a delightful twist.

PREP TIME:
3 MINUTES

COOK TIME:
4 TO 5 MINUTES

Tips

For added flavor, drizzle a little of the oil that the sun-dried tomatoes are packed in onto your English muffin.

Fontina is considered one of the most versatile cheeses, great both in cooking and for serving as is. The flavor adds a wonderfully tart, nutty and buttery taste to your sandwich.

I buy sliced ripe olives in 4-oz (125 mL) cans to use in this sandwich, then store the remainder in an airtight container in the refrigerator to use in other recipes.

◆ Preheat breakfast sandwich maker

1	multigrain English muffin, split in half	1
1 tbsp	chopped drained oil-packed sun-dried tomatoes	15 mL
1 tbsp	sliced black olives	15 mL
1	slice fontina cheese	1
	Nonstick cooking spray	
1	large egg	1

1. Place one English muffin half, split side up, in bottom ring of sandwich maker. Top with sun-dried tomatoes, olives and cheese.

2. Lower the cooking plate and top ring. Lightly spray the plate with cooking spray, then crack the egg into the ring. Pierce top of egg yolk with a toothpick or plastic fork. Place the other muffin half, split side down, on top of the egg.

3. Gently close the cover and cook for 4 to 5 minutes or until egg is cooked to your liking. Rotate cooking plate away from sandwich maker and lift rings. Use a plastic or nylon spatula to remove the sandwich. Serve immediately.

Variation

Kalamata olive spread makes for a nice alternative to the black olives. Spread $1\frac{1}{2}$ tsp (7 mL) on the split side of the bottom muffin half before placing the muffin half in the ring.

Hummus and Veggies on Pita

If you enjoy hummus as an appetizer or snack, you will really appreciate the flavor of the Middle Eastern spread in a flavorful breakfast sandwich.

<table>
<tr><td>PREP TIME:
2 MINUTES</td></tr>
</table>

<table>
<tr><td>COOK TIME:
4 TO 5 MINUTES</td></tr>
</table>

Tips

Hummus can be found in the deli or produce section of your grocery store.

Enjoy leftover hummus as a midday snack with flatbread or pita slices for dipping.

* Preheat breakfast sandwich maker

2 tbsp	hummus	30 mL
1	small pita, cut into a 4-inch (10 cm) round and split in half horizontally	1
2	slices cucumber	2
1	slice tomato	1
	Nonstick cooking spray	
1	large egg	1
2 tsp	sliced black olives (optional)	10 mL

1. Spread hummus on split side of each pita half. Place one pita half, spread side up, in bottom ring of sandwich maker. Top with cucumber and tomato.

2. Lower the cooking plate and top ring. Lightly spray the plate with cooking spray, then crack the egg into the ring. Pierce top of egg yolk with a toothpick or plastic fork. Sprinkle with olives (if using). Place the other pita half, spread side down, on top of the egg.

3. Gently close the cover and cook for 4 to 5 minutes or until egg is cooked to your liking. Rotate cooking plate away from sandwich maker and lift rings. Use a plastic or nylon spatula to remove the sandwich. Serve immediately.

Variation

Sprinkle a few pine nuts on top of the veggies for added crunch, flavor and texture.

Black Bean and Pepper Jack Sandwich

The combination of pepper Jack cheese, black beans and salsa makes for a tasty Mexican-inspired sandwich that will give you a spicy kick for breakfast or any time of day.

PREP TIME:
3 MINUTES

COOK TIME:
4 TO 5 MINUTES

Tips

Leftover black beans can be used as a side dish, along with rice, for many Mexican or Cuban dishes. I also like to use black beans in enchiladas, breakfast burritos or on top of a taco salad.

This sandwich gets a little gooey with the beans and salsa, so it might be best to eat it with a fork.

◆ Preheat breakfast sandwich maker

1	English muffin, split in half	1
1	slice pepper Jack cheese	1
2 tbsp	rinsed drained canned black beans	30 mL
1 tbsp	salsa	15 mL
	Nonstick cooking spray	
1	large egg	1

1. Place one English muffin half, split side up, in bottom ring of sandwich maker. Top with cheese, beans and salsa.

2. Lower the cooking plate and top ring. Lightly spray the plate with cooking spray, then crack the egg into the ring. Pierce top of egg yolk with a toothpick or plastic fork. Place the other muffin half, split side down, on top of the egg.

3. Gently close the cover and cook for 4 to 5 minutes or until egg is cooked to your liking. Rotate cooking plate away from sandwich maker and lift rings. Use a plastic or nylon spatula to remove the sandwich. Serve immediately.

Stuffed Portobello Mushroom

Topped with creamy goat cheese, a portobello mushroom makes a delightful meatless breakfast sandwich.

PREP TIME:

3 MINUTES

COOK TIME:

4 TO 5 MINUTES

Tips

Chèvre cheese is made from goat's milk. It is ideal for some individuals with a low tolerance to cow's milk.

If you like your arugula crisp and cool, wait to add it until after removing the sandwich from the sandwich maker.

Variation

Try using chèvre flavored with garlic chives, herbes de Provence or black truffle.

◆ Preheat breakfast sandwich maker

1	portobello mushroom cap (about 4 inches/10 cm in diameter), stem and gills removed	1
Pinch	ground sage	Pinch
Pinch	salt	Pinch
Pinch	freshly ground black pepper (optional)	Pinch
1	medium slice soft chèvre cheese	1
	Olive oil	
	Nonstick cooking spray	
1	large egg	1
¼ cup	arugula	60 mL

1. Sprinkle the inside of the mushroom cap with sage, salt and pepper (if using), then spread with cheese.

2. Add a small drop of olive oil to bottom ring of sandwich maker. Place filled portobello cap in ring.

3. Lower the cooking plate and top ring. Lightly spray the plate with cooking spray, then crack the egg into the ring. Pierce top of egg yolk with a toothpick or plastic fork. Place arugula on top of the egg.

4. Gently close the cover and cook for 4 to 5 minutes or until egg is cooked to your liking. Rotate cooking plate away from sandwich maker and lift rings. Use a plastic or nylon spatula to remove the sandwich. Serve immediately.

Portobello Mushroom Burger

Whether you are a vegetarian or just like to enjoy a meatless meal occasionally, this portobello mushroom burger offers the flavor and texture of a traditional beef burger.

PREP TIME:
4 MINUTES

COOK TIME:
4 TO 5 MINUTES

Tip

If you have time to marinate the portobello in the Italian dressing for 30 to 60 minutes before preparing your sandwich, the mushroom will be more tender and the flavors intensified.

Variation

For a richer and creamier sandwich, use slices of the cherry-size fresh mozzarella known as ciliegine, or the slightly larger, 1¾-oz (50 g) balls of fresh mozzarella called bocconcini.

♦ Preheat breakfast sandwich maker

1	portobello mushroom cap (about 4 inches/10 cm in diameter), stem and gills removed	1
2 tbsp	Italian salad dressing	30 mL
1	4-inch (10 cm) burger bun, split in half	1
1	roasted red bell pepper, cut into strips	1
1	slice provolone cheese	1
¼ cup	arugula	60 mL

1. Place mushroom cap in a small bowl and drizzle with Italian dressing. Set aside.

2. Place bottom half of bun in bottom ring of sandwich maker. Top with roasted pepper and cheese.

3. Lower the cooking plate and ring. Remove mushroom cap from dressing, discarding excess dressing, and place the mushroom, gill side up, in the ring.

4. Gently close the cover and cook for 4 to 5 minutes or until mushroom is cooked to your liking. Rotate cooking plate away from sandwich maker and lift rings. Use a plastic or nylon spatula to remove the sandwich.

5. Top with arugula and top half of bun. Serve immediately.

Margherita Pizza

Sometimes the simplest things taste the best, like this super-easy and light pizza. It's great for a quick treat on a hot day.

PREP TIME:
2 MINUTES

COOK TIME:
2 TO 3 MINUTES

Tips

Look for small ready-made pizza crusts and pizza sauce in the Italian or deli section of your grocery store. The crusts come in multiples, often in a resealable bag, so you'll have more on hand for your pizza cravings.

If you are not able to find small pizza crusts, cut a larger crust into a 4-inch (10 cm) round using a cookie cutter, kitchen scissors or the top of a wide-mouth canning jar ring.

◆ Preheat breakfast sandwich maker

1	4-inch (10 cm) ready-made pizza crust (see tips, at left)	1
1½ tsp	olive oil	7 mL
2 tbsp	pizza sauce	30 mL
2 tbsp	shredded mozzarella cheese	30 mL
1 tbsp	freshly grated Parmesan cheese (optional)	15 mL

1. Brush both sides of pizza crust with olive oil. Place crust in bottom ring of sandwich maker. Spread pizza sauce over crust. Sprinkle with mozzarella.

2. Lower the cooking plate and top ring. Close the cover and cook for 2 to 3 minutes or until mozzarella is melted and crust edges are brown. Rotate cooking plate away from sandwich maker and lift rings. Use a plastic or nylon spatula to remove the pizza.

3. Let stand for 1 minute to allow mozzarella to set. Sprinkle with Parmesan, if desired. Serve immediately.

Roasted Red Pepper and Mushroom Omelet

Roasted red peppers add color, texture and sweetness to this tasty omelet. The mushrooms add a slight earthy flavor.

PREP TIME:
5 MINUTES

COOK TIME:
3 TO 4 MINUTES

Tips

You can purchase roasted red bell peppers in glass jars at your local grocery store. They make a great addition to any pasta dish or sandwich.

Canned or fresh mushrooms work equally well in this omelet, but I prefer canned for their consistency and ease of use.

I typically use button mushrooms in this recipe, as they are so readily available, but any of your favorite varieties will work well.

♦ Preheat breakfast sandwich maker

1	large egg	1
2 tbsp	diced drained canned or fresh mushrooms	30 mL
1 tbsp	finely chopped roasted red bell pepper	15 mL
Pinch	salt (optional)	Pinch
Pinch	freshly ground black pepper (optional)	Pinch
	Nonstick cooking spray	

1. In a small bowl, gently whisk egg. Stir in mushrooms and roasted pepper. Season with salt and pepper (if using).

2. Lower the cooking plate and both rings of sandwich maker. Lightly spray the cooking plate with cooking spray. Pour the egg mixture into the top ring.

3. Gently close the cover and cook for 3 to 4 minutes or until omelet is cooked to your liking. Rotate cooking plate away from sandwich maker and lift rings. Use a plastic or nylon spatula to remove the omelet. Serve immediately.

Variation

Add 1 tbsp (15 mL) diced zucchini for more color.

Baby Spinach and Mushroom Omelet

Popeye loved to eat spinach to build his muscles, and he was on to something, as this leafy green vegetable offers numerous beneficial nutrients. Adding spinach to your breakfast is a healthy way to start your day.

PREP TIME:
5 MINUTES

COOK TIME:
3 TO 4 MINUTES

Tips

Use 2 egg whites, instead of the whole egg, if you are looking to reduce your cholesterol intake. The yolk contains most of the fat and cholesterol, but keep in mind that it also supplies most of the nutrients, such as vitamins A and D, phosphorus, folate and calcium.

Add some of the remaining spinach to a green smoothie or a power-packed salad for lunch.

♦ Preheat breakfast sandwich maker

1	large egg	1
1 tbsp	diced mushrooms	15 mL
2 tbsp	chopped baby spinach	30 mL
1 tbsp	freshly grated Parmesan cheese	15 mL
Pinch	salt (optional)	Pinch
Pinch	freshly ground black pepper (optional)	Pinch
	Nonstick cooking spray	

1. In a small bowl, gently whisk egg. Stir in mushrooms, spinach and cheese. Season with salt and pepper (if using).

2. Lower the cooking plate and both rings of sandwich maker. Lightly spray the cooking plate with cooking spray. Pour the egg mixture into the top ring.

3. Gently close the cover and cook for 3 to 4 minutes or until omelet is cooked to your liking. Rotate cooking plate away from sandwich maker and lift rings. Use a plastic or nylon spatula to remove the omelet. Serve immediately.

Variation

Replace the Parmesan with Romano or aged Asiago cheese. Aged Asiago has a stronger flavor and a harder texture than its fresher counterpart. If you use aged Asiago for this recipe, shave it instead of grating it.

Sautéed Kale and Onion Frittata

Pair the slightly tangy and bitter taste of kale with the sweetness of sautéed onions and you have a rich, full-flavored breakfast bonanza. The smell of sautéing onions always arouses my early morning taste buds.

PREP TIME:
25 MINUTES

COOK TIME:
3 TO 4 MINUTES PER FRITTATA

Tips

This recipe makes two frittatas because of the extra preparation time involved. Share one of these healthy frittatas with someone or enjoy both yourself.

Young kale works best in this recipe, as it will wilt better when sautéed.

Variations

Add a pinch of diced garlic with the onions to add even more flavor to this frittata.

Use olive or coconut oil in place of the butter. Or compromise by using 1 tbsp (15 mL) oil and 1 tbsp (15 mL) butter.

◆ Preheat breakfast sandwich maker

2 tbsp	butter	30 mL
½ cup	chopped onion	125 mL
1 cup	chopped stemmed kale	250 mL
2	large eggs	2
1	large egg white	1
2 tbsp	shredded Asiago cheese	30 mL
Pinch	salt (optional)	Pinch
Pinch	freshly ground black pepper (optional)	Pinch
	Nonstick cooking spray	

1. In a small skillet, melt butter over low heat. Add onions and cook, stirring, for about 10 minutes or until translucent. Add kale, increase heat to medium-high and cook, stirring, for about 5 minutes or until onions are golden brown and kale is wilted.

2. In a small bowl, whisk together eggs, egg white and cheese. Stir in onion and kale mixture.

3. Lower the cooking plate and both rings of sandwich maker. Lightly spray the cooking plate with cooking spray. Pour half of the egg mixture into the top ring.

4. Gently close the cover and cook for 3 to 4 minutes or until frittata is cooked to your liking. Rotate cooking plate away from sandwich maker and lift rings. Use a plastic or nylon spatula to remove the frittata. Serve immediately.

5. Repeat steps 3 and 4 with the remaining egg mixture.

Gluten-Free Options

✕✕✕✕✕✕✕✕✕✕✕✕✕✕✕✕✕✕✕✕✕✕✕✕✕✕✕✕✕✕✕✕✕✕✕✕✕✕✕

Sweet Peach and Chia on Flaxseed Bread

Power-packed with flax and chia seeds, and sweet with peaches, this sandwich is a delight at any time of the day.

PREP TIME:

3 MINUTES

COOK TIME:

4 TO 5 MINUTES

Tips

You can use peaches from a 4-oz (113 mL) fruit cup instead of fresh peaches. Use about half the cup for your sandwich and enjoy the remainder as a side of fruit.

Pears and apples also work very nicely in this sandwich. These fruits are also available in ready-to-eat fruit cups.

♦ Preheat breakfast sandwich maker

2 tbsp	yogurt	30 mL
2	slices gluten-free flaxseed bread, cut into 4-inch (10 cm) rounds	2
½	peach, cut into slices	½
1 tbsp	chia seeds	15 mL
	Nonstick cooking spray	
1	large egg	1

1. Spread yogurt on one side of each bread slice. Place one slice, spread side up, in bottom ring of sandwich maker. Top with peaches and sprinkle with chia seeds.

2. Lower the cooking plate and top ring. Lightly spray the plate with cooking spray, then crack the egg into the ring. Pierce top of egg yolk with a toothpick or plastic fork. Place the other bread slice, spread side down, on top of the egg.

3. Gently close the cover and cook for 4 to 5 minutes or until egg is cooked to your liking. Rotate cooking plate away from sandwich maker and lift rings. Use a plastic or nylon spatula to remove the sandwich. Serve immediately.

Scrambled Egg and Cheddar Sandwich

Scrambled eggs are one of my favorite breakfast dishes. With the breakfast sandwich maker, you can enjoy them in less time, and with less mess.

PREP TIME:
3 MINUTES

COOK TIME:
4 TO 5 MINUTES

Tips

When buying shredded Cheddar cheese, make sure there is no added gluten. Cheese manufacturers often add flour to keep the cheese pieces from sticking together.

Whenever possible, shred your own Cheddar cheese, as it tastes so much fresher. I always keep a block of Cheddar in the refrigerator because I use it in so many dishes.

◆ Preheat breakfast sandwich maker

1	large egg	1
1 tbsp	chopped green onion	15 mL
2	slices gluten-free bread, cut into 4-inch (10 cm) rounds	2
1 tbsp	shredded Cheddar cheese	15 mL
	Nonstick cooking spray	

1. In a small bowl, gently whisk egg. Stir in green onion. Set aside.

2. Place one bread slice in bottom ring of sandwich maker. Top with cheese.

3. Lower the cooking plate and top ring. Lightly spray the plate with cooking spray, then pour in the egg mixture. Place the other bread slice on top of the egg.

4. Gently close the cover and cook for 4 to 5 minutes or until egg is cooked to your liking. Rotate cooking plate away from sandwich maker and lift rings. Use a plastic or nylon spatula to remove the sandwich. Serve immediately.

Bacon, Cheese and Tomato Sandwich

Another take on a classic breakfast sandwich, with tomato for a touch of sunshine.

PREP TIME:

2 MINUTES

COOK TIME:

4 TO 5 MINUTES

Tip

If you are buying sliced cheese that has been packaged at the factory, check the label for any packaging agents that may include gluten. Cheese that has been sliced at your local deli is at risk of cross-contamination with other products in the deli that contain gluten. For the best results, buy your cheese in blocks and slice it yourself.

• Preheat breakfast sandwich maker

2	slices gluten-free bread, cut into 4-inch (10 cm) rounds	2
1	slice Monterey Jack cheese	1
2	slices bacon, cooked crisp	2
1	slice tomato	1
	Nonstick cooking spray	
1	large egg	1
2 tsp	chopped black olives (optional)	10 mL

1. Place one bread slice in bottom ring of sandwich maker. Top with cheese, bacon and tomato.

2. Lower the cooking plate and top ring. Lightly spray the plate with cooking spray, then crack the egg into the ring. Pierce top of egg yolk with a toothpick or plastic fork. Sprinkle with black olives (if using). Place the other bread slice on top of the egg.

3. Gently close the cover and cook for 4 to 5 minutes or until egg is cooked to your liking. Rotate cooking plate away from sandwich maker and lift rings. Use a plastic or nylon spatula to remove the sandwich. Serve immediately.

Classic Canadian Bacon and
Cheddar Sandwich (page 14)

Florentine Sandwich (page 33)

Chicken Club Sandwich (page 53)

Artichoke, Roasted Pepper
and Ricotta Frittata (page 57)

The Classic Cheeseburger (page 69)

**Apple, Sausage and Cheddar
Croissant (page 87)**

Bacon, Avocado and Swiss on Quinoa Bread

If you haven't tried quinoa bread, now is a good time to start. It is moist and has a slightly nutty texture, making for a great sandwich.

PREP TIME:
2 MINUTES

COOK TIME:
4 TO 5 MINUTES

Tips

When purchasing avocados, choose those that give when pressed gently but firmly with your thumb. The color will not always correctly indicate how ripe the avocado is.

If your avocado isn't ripe enough to spread, you can use the slice of avocado instead.

◆ Preheat breakfast sandwich maker

1	slice very ripe avocado	1
2	slices quinoa bread, cut into 4-inch (10 cm) rounds	2
1	slice Swiss cheese	1
3	slices bacon, cooked crisp	3
	Nonstick cooking spray	
1	large egg	1

1. Spread avocado on one side of a bread slice. Place slice, spread side up, in bottom ring of sandwich maker. Top with cheese. Break bacon into pieces that fit in the ring and add on top of the cheese.

2. Lower the cooking plate and top ring. Lightly spray the plate with cooking spray, then crack the egg into the ring. Pierce top of egg yolk with a toothpick or plastic fork. Place the other bread slice on top of the egg.

3. Gently close the cover and cook for 4 to 5 minutes or until egg is cooked to your liking. Rotate cooking plate away from sandwich maker and lift rings. Use a plastic or nylon spatula to remove the sandwich. Serve immediately.

Sausage and Egg on a Biscuit

A warm biscuit with sausage and egg makes for a nice comfort food breakfast sandwich.

Tips

Serve with a cup of fresh fruit on the side for a well-rounded breakfast.

If purchasing sliced cheese, check the package to be sure it does not contain gluten.

◆ Preheat breakfast sandwich maker

1	gluten-free biscuit, split in half	1
1	slice Colby cheese	1
1	frozen cooked gluten-free pork sausage patty	1
	Nonstick cooking spray	
1	large egg	1
1 tbsp	chopped fresh basil (optional)	15 mL

1. Place one biscuit half, split side up, in bottom ring of sandwich maker. Top with cheese and sausage.

2. Lower the cooking plate and top ring. Lightly spray the plate with cooking spray, then crack the egg into the ring. Pierce top of egg yolk with a toothpick or plastic fork. Sprinkle with basil (if using). Place the other biscuit half, split side down, on top of the egg.

3. Gently close the cover and cook for 4 to 5 minutes or until egg is cooked to your liking. Rotate cooking plate away from sandwich maker and lift rings. Use a plastic or nylon spatula to remove the sandwich. Serve immediately.

Variations

You can use a pinch of dried basil in place of fresh.

Use Cheddar or Monterey Jack instead of Colby cheese.

Sausage, Cheese and Egg White Sandwich

Now that gluten-free English muffins are more commonly available in stores, you can enjoy a classic breakfast sandwich at home.

PREP TIME:
1 MINUTE

COOK TIME:
3 TO 4 MINUTES

Tips

When purchasing frozen sausage patties, check the package to make sure they are gluten-free. There are many great brands that do not contain gluten.

If your grocer's meat section sells fresh cooked sausage patties, feel free to use one of those instead.

◆ Preheat breakfast sandwich maker

1	gluten-free English muffin, split in half	1
1 tbsp	shredded sharp (old) Cheddar cheese	15 mL
1	frozen cooked gluten-free pork sausage patty	1
	Nonstick cooking spray	
1	large egg white	1

1. Place one English muffin half, split side up, in bottom ring of sandwich maker. Top with cheese and sausage.

2. Lower the cooking plate and top ring. Lightly spray the plate with cooking spray, then add the egg white. Place the other muffin half, split side down, on top of the egg white.

3. Gently close the cover and cook for 3 to 4 minutes or until egg white is cooked through and no longer translucent. Rotate cooking plate away from sandwich maker and lift rings. Use a plastic or nylon spatula to remove the sandwich. Serve immediately.

Prosciutto and Scrambled Egg Sandwich

The combination of prosciutto, scrambled eggs and mushrooms makes for a breakfast sandwich full of delicate flavor.

Tip

Use drained canned mushroom pieces and stems to make preparation easier. Store the remainder in an airtight container in the refrigerator for up to 1 week.

◆ Preheat breakfast sandwich maker

1	large egg	1
1 tbsp	chopped drained canned or fresh mushrooms	15 mL
1	gluten-free English muffin, split in half	1
1 tbsp	shredded Asiago cheese	15 mL
2 to 3	thin slices prosciutto	2 to 3
	Nonstick cooking spray	

1. In a small bowl, gently whisk egg. Stir in mushrooms. Set aside.

2. Place one English muffin half, split side up, in bottom ring of sandwich maker. Top with cheese and prosciutto.

3. Lower the cooking plate and top ring. Lightly spray the plate with cooking spray, then pour in the egg mixture. Place the other muffin half, split side down, on top of the egg.

4. Gently close the cover and cook for 4 to 5 minutes or until egg is cooked to your liking. Rotate cooking plate away from sandwich maker and lift rings. Use a plastic or nylon spatula to remove the sandwich. Serve immediately.

Chicken Club Sandwich

This sandwich is much like the classic chicken club, but made with an egg so you can enjoy it for breakfast (or any time of day).

PREP TIME:
3 MINUTES

COOK TIME:
4 TO 5 MINUTES

Tip

You can purchase cooked bacon or cook up your own ahead of time to use in all of your breakfast sandwiches or to add as a topping to salads.

♦ Preheat breakfast sandwich maker

	Gluten-free mayonnaise (optional)	
2	slices gluten-free bread, cut into 4-inch (10 cm) rounds	2
2	slices deli roasted chicken	2
1	slice provolone cheese	1
1	slice tomato	1
1	slice bacon, cooked crisp	1
	Nonstick cooking spray	
1	large egg	1

1. If desired, spread mayonnaise on one side of each bread slice. Place one slice, spread side up, in bottom ring of sandwich maker. Top with chicken, cheese and tomato. Break bacon into pieces that fit in the ring and place on top of the tomato.

2. Lower the cooking plate and top ring. Lightly spray the plate with cooking spray, then crack the egg into the ring. Pierce top of egg yolk with a toothpick or plastic fork. Place the other bread slice, spread side down, on top of the egg.

3. Gently close the cover and cook for 4 to 5 minutes or until egg is cooked to your liking. Rotate cooking plate away from sandwich maker and lift rings. Use a plastic or nylon spatula to remove the sandwich. Serve immediately.

Variation

Use 2 egg whites, instead of the whole egg, if you are looking to reduce your cholesterol intake. The yolk contains most of the fat and cholesterol, but keep in mind that it also supplies most of the nutrients, such as vitamins A and D, phosphorus, folate and calcium.

Chicken Breast and Edam Sandwich

Here, chicken and Edam, with its buttery, slightly caramel flavor, are topped with green apples for an autumn sandwich that is both lean and delicious.

PREP TIME:

2 MINUTES

COOK TIME:

4 TO 5 MINUTES

Tips

You can use either leftover cooked chicken breast or sliced deli chicken.

Green apples give this sandwich a bit of extra tartness and stay a bit firmer than their red counterparts. But if you prefer red apples, they will work fine here.

Fun fact: Edam was originally shaped into balls so the Dutch could roll it down the planks of ships for export.

◆ Preheat breakfast sandwich maker

1	4-inch (20 cm) gluten-free bun, split in half	1
2	slices cooked chicken breast	2
1	slice Edam cheese	1
¼	green apple, sliced	¼
	Nonstick cooking spray	
1	large egg	1
Pinch	dried sage (optional)	Pinch
Pinch	dried fennel leaf (optional)	Pinch

1. Place one bun half, split side up, in bottom ring of sandwich maker. Top with chicken, cheese and apple.

2. Lower the cooking plate and top ring. Lightly spray the plate with cooking spray, then crack the egg into the ring. Pierce top of egg yolk with a toothpick or plastic fork. Sprinkle with sage and fennel (if using). Place the other bun half, split side down, on top of the egg.

3. Gently close the cover and cook for 4 to 5 minutes or until egg is cooked to your liking. Rotate cooking plate away from sandwich maker and lift rings. Use a plastic or nylon spatula to remove the sandwich. Serve immediately.

Mushroom Quiche on a Turkey Sausage Crust

I love that you can make quiche without a crust in the sandwich maker. A turkey sausage patty works beautifully as a substitute.

PREP TIME:
2 MINUTES

COOK TIME:
4 TO 5 MINUTES

Tip

Sausage patties are often smaller in diameter than the bottom ring of the sandwich maker, so make sure no edges of the cheese fall over the edge of the patty, or the cheese will melt down onto the sandwich plate.

• Preheat breakfast sandwich maker

1	large egg	1
1 tbsp	chopped mushrooms	15 mL
1	frozen cooked gluten-free turkey sausage patty	1
1	slice Swiss cheese	1
	Nonstick cooking spray	

1. In a small bowl, gently whisk egg. Stir in mushrooms. Set aside.

2. Place sausage in bottom ring of sandwich maker. Top with cheese.

3. Lower the cooking plate and top ring. Lightly spray the plate with cooking spray, then pour in the egg mixture.

4. Gently close the cover and cook for 4 to 5 minutes or until egg is cooked to your liking. Rotate cooking plate away from sandwich maker and lift rings. Use a plastic or nylon spatula to remove the quiche. Serve immediately.

Variations

Add 1 tbsp (15 mL) chopped onion to the egg mixture.

A frozen cooked gluten-free pork sausage patty would be a nice alternative to the turkey sausage.

Herb and Onion Frittata

This simple yet flavorful breakfast dish features Italian flavors and fewer carbohydrates than you'd get in a breakfast sandwich.

PREP TIME:

2 MINUTES

COOK TIME:

5 TO 7 MINUTES

Tip

If you prefer, you can eliminate the step of cooking the onion. Just stir the chopped onion into the egg mixture. The onion will be firmer and will have a little more bite.

• Preheat breakfast sandwich maker

1	large egg	1
2 tsp	dried Italian seasoning	10 mL
Pinch	salt (optional)	Pinch
Pinch	freshly ground black pepper (optional)	Pinch
1 tsp	coconut or olive oil	5 mL
2 tbsp	chopped onion	30 mL

1. In a small bowl, gently whisk egg. Stir in Italian seasoning. Season with salt and pepper (if using). Set aside.

2. Lower the cooking plate and both rings of sandwich maker. Add coconut oil to the cooking plate and let it melt slightly. Add onion, close the cover and cook, stirring occasionally with a small rubber spatula or plastic spoon, for 2 to 3 minutes or until onion is almost translucent. Pour the egg mixture on top of the onion.

3. Gently close the cover and cook for 3 to 4 minutes or until frittata is cooked to your liking. Rotate cooking plate away from sandwich maker and lift rings. Use a plastic or nylon spatula to remove the frittata. Serve immediately.

Artichoke, Roasted Pepper and Ricotta Frittata

The combination of artichokes, roasted peppers and ricotta makes this frittata taste like a decadent appetizer served up on the Italian coast.

PREP TIME:
3 MINUTES

COOK TIME:
3 TO 4 MINUTES

Tip

Ricotta is available in a range of fat options, from nonfat to whole milk.

◆ Preheat breakfast sandwich maker

1	large egg	1
3 tbsp	chopped drained oil-packed or marinated artichoke hearts	45 mL
1	roasted red bell pepper, chopped	1
1 tbsp	ricotta cheese	15 mL
Pinch	salt (optional)	Pinch
	Nonstick cooking spray	

1. In a small bowl, gently whisk egg. Stir in artichoke hearts, roasted peppers and cheese. Season with salt (if using).

2. Lower the cooking plate and both rings of sandwich maker. Lightly spray the cooking plate with cooking spray. Pour the egg mixture into the top ring.

3. Gently close the cover and cook for 3 to 4 minutes or until frittata is cooked to your liking. Rotate cooking plate away from sandwich maker and lift rings. Use a plastic or nylon spatula to remove the frittata. Serve immediately.

Variation

Crumbled feta cheese is a nice alternative to ricotta in this recipe. Feta has a tarter and saltier taste, so you likely won't want to add the pinch of salt.

Beef Sandwiches and Burgers

◇◇◇◇◇◇◇◇◇◇◇◇◇◇◇◇◇◇◇◇◇◇◇◇◇◇◇◇◇◇◇◇◇◇◇◇◇

BBQ Beef Breakfast Sandwich

The sweet and tangy flavors in this sandwich make it a great meal any time of day.

PREP TIME:

2 MINUTES

COOK TIME:

4 TO 5 MINUTES

Tip

Pulled barbecued beef can be purchased in tubs or packages at the grocery store. There will be enough servings in the tub to make more sandwiches for busy days. Alternatively you can use leftovers from a roast or steak (freeze individual portions for easy sandwich making) with a dollop of barbecue sauce to taste.

♦ Preheat breakfast sandwich maker

1 tbsp	pickle relish	15 mL
1	4-inch (10 cm) sandwich bun, split in half	1
2/3 cup	pulled barbecued beef	150 mL
	Nonstick cooking spray	
1	large egg	1
2	rings red onion	2

1. Spread relish on split side of bottom half of bun. Place bun half, spread side up, in bottom ring of sandwich maker. Top with beef.

2. Lower the cooking plate and top ring. Lightly spray the plate with cooking spray, then crack the egg into the ring. Pierce top of egg yolk with a toothpick or plastic fork. Top with onion rings. Place the other bun half, split side down, on top of the egg.

3. Gently close the cover and cook for 4 to 5 minutes or until egg is cooked to your liking. Rotate cooking plate away from sandwich maker and lift rings. Use a plastic or nylon spatula to remove the sandwich. Serve immediately.

Leftover Pot Roast Sandwich

Just one more reason to make extra pot roast: so you can enjoy it with your favorite sandwich fixings.

PREP TIME:
3 MINUTES

COOK TIME:
4 TO 5 MINUTES

Tips

This recipe calls for some of the traditional pot roast ingredients — onions and carrots — but be careful not to overload your sandwich. You do not want the vegetables to be mashed up against the top of the egg plate.

If you prefer, just add the roasted onions to your sandwich and serve the carrots on the side.

♦ Preheat breakfast sandwich maker

1	4-inch (10 cm) sandwich bun, split in half	1
1	slice mild Cheddar cheese	1
2	small slices leftover beef pot roast	2
	Cooked carrots (left over from pot roast)	
	Cooked onions (left over from pot roast)	
	Nonstick cooking spray	
1	large egg	1

1. Place bottom half of bun, split side up, in bottom ring of sandwich maker. Top with cheese, beef and a few carrots and onions.

2. Lower the cooking plate and top ring. Lightly spray the plate with cooking spray, then crack the egg into the ring. Pierce top of egg yolk with a toothpick or plastic fork. Place the other bun half, split side down, on top of the egg.

3. Gently close the cover and cook for 4 to 5 minutes or until egg is cooked to your liking. Rotate cooking plate away from sandwich maker and lift rings. Use a plastic or nylon spatula to remove the sandwich. Serve immediately.

Roast Beef and Blue Cheese Sandwich

The sweetness of the apricot preserves complements the blue cheese and roast beef, giving this sandwich a robust flavor.

PREP TIME:

2 MINUTES

COOK TIME:

4 TO 5 MINUTES

Tip

You can use leftovers from a roast or steak in place of the deli roast beef. Freeze individual portions for easy sandwich making.

◆ Preheat breakfast sandwich maker

1 tbsp	apricot preserves	15 mL
1	4-inch (10 cm) sandwich bun, split in half	1
2 to 3	slices deli roast beef	2 to 3
2 tbsp	crumbled blue cheese	30 mL
	Nonstick cooking spray	
1	large egg	1

1. Spread preserves on split side of bottom half of bun. Place bun half, spread side up, in bottom ring of sandwich maker. Top with beef and cheese.

2. Lower the cooking plate and top ring. Lightly spray the plate with cooking spray, then crack the egg into the ring. Pierce top of egg yolk with a toothpick or plastic fork. Place the other bun half, split side down, on top of the egg.

3. Gently close the cover and cook for 4 to 5 minutes or until egg is cooked to your liking Rotate cooking plate away from sandwich maker and lift rings. Use a plastic or nylon spatula to remove the sandwich. Serve immediately.

Variations

Use 2 dried apricots instead of the apricot preserves. They will add a little more texture, but will not have as robust a flavor.

For a zestier flavor, use orange marmalade in place of the apricot preserves.

Hot Pastrami on Rye

A true deli favorite, this type of sandwich is often packed with so much pastrami you can barely take a bite. Mine is still loaded with flavor, but is a little easier to eat.

PREP TIME:
2 MINUTES

COOK TIME:
4 TO 5 MINUTES

Tips

Pastrami is similar to corned beef in that it has been salt-cured, but, unlike corned beef, pastrami has also been smoked.

This sandwich has a high sodium content, so limit your sodium intake in your other meals for the day. Or omit the pickles and capers to lower the sodium of this sandwich.

◆ Preheat breakfast sandwich maker

2	slices rye bread, cut into 4-inch (10 cm) rounds	2
2 to 3	slices deli pastrami	2 to 3
1	slice Swiss cheese	1
2	slices pickle	2
	Nonstick cooking spray	
1	large egg	1
1	ring red onion (optional)	1
1 tsp	drained capers (optional)	5 mL

1. Place one bread slice in bottom ring of sandwich maker. Top with pastrami, cheese and pickles.

2. Lower the cooking plate and top ring. Lightly spray the plate with cooking spray, then crack the egg into the ring. Pierce top of egg yolk with a toothpick or plastic fork. Top with onion ring and capers (if using). Place the other bread slice on top of the egg.

3. Gently close the cover and cook for 4 to 5 minutes or until egg is cooked to your liking. Rotate cooking plate away from sandwich maker and lift rings. Use a plastic or nylon spatula to remove the sandwich. Serve immediately.

Corned Beef and Swiss on Pumpernickel

Corned beef is a salt-cured or brined beef typically made from the brisket cut. This sandwich is my take on a delicatessen favorite.

PREP TIME:

2 MINUTES

COOK TIME:

4 TO 5 MINUTES

Tips

Use a round cookie cutter, the metal ring of a wide-mouth canning jar or kitchen shears to cut your pumpernickel bread into 4-inch (10 cm) rounds.

Make sure the cheese fits nicely on top of the bread and doesn't extend beyond the edges, so it doesn't melt all over the inside of your sandwich maker.

◆ Preheat breakfast sandwich maker

2 tsp	Thousand Island dressing	10 mL
2	slices pumpernickel bread, cut into 4-inch (10 cm) rounds	2
2 to 3	slices deli corned beef	2 to 3
1	slice Swiss cheese	1
	Nonstick cooking spray	
1	large egg	1

1. Spread dressing on one side of each bread slice. Place one slice, spread side up, in bottom ring of sandwich maker. Top with beef and cheese.

2. Lower the cooking plate and top ring. Lightly spray the plate with cooking spray, then crack the egg into the ring. Pierce top of egg yolk with a toothpick or plastic fork. Place the other bread slice, spread side down, on top of the egg.

3. Gently close the cover and cook for 4 to 5 minutes or until egg is cooked to your liking. Rotate cooking plate away from sandwich maker and lift rings. Use a plastic or nylon spatula to remove the sandwich. Serve immediately.

Variations

Use any tangy salad dressing in place of the Thousand Island dressing. You may also want to add some pickle relish to replicate the traditional flavors.

For a richer, slightly sweeter taste, use balsamic vinaigrette in place of the Thousand Island dressing. Add some pickle slices to retain the tangy flavor and crunch.

Reuben Breakfast Sandwich

The origins of the Reuben sandwich have been obscured over the decades, but one thing is for sure: this sandwich is beloved by many.

PREP TIME:

2 MINUTES

COOK TIME:

4 TO 5 MINUTES

Tip

Bavarian sauerkraut, made with caraway seeds, is a nice alternative to regular sauerkraut.

* Preheat breakfast sandwich maker

2 tsp	Russian dressing	10 mL
2	slices rye bread, cut into 4-inch (10 cm) rounds	2
1	slice Swiss cheese	1
2 to 3	slices deli corned beef	2 to 3
2 tbsp	drained sauerkraut	30 mL
	Nonstick cooking spray	
1	large egg	1

1. Spread dressing on one side of each bread slice. Place one slice, spread side up, in bottom ring of sandwich maker. Top with cheese, beef and sauerkraut.

2. Lower the cooking plate and top ring. Lightly spray the plate with cooking spray, then crack the egg into the ring. Pierce top of egg yolk with a toothpick or plastic fork. Place the other bread slice, spread side down, on top of the egg.

3. Gently close the cover and cook for 4 to 5 minutes or until egg is cooked to your liking. Rotate cooking plate away from sandwich maker and lift rings. Use a plastic or nylon spatula to remove the sandwich. Serve immediately.

Variation

An English muffin can be substituted for the rye bread. While rye or pumpernickel bread is traditional for a Reuben, an English muffin tastes equally good.

Corned Beef and Gruyère Sandwich

Gruyère, a semi-hard cheese, gives this sandwich a nutty, full-flavored taste.

PREP TIME:

2 MINUTES

COOK TIME:

4 TO 5 MINUTES

Tip

I like to use kosher pickle slices in this sandwich, to keep with the delicatessen style, but any type of pickle slices will work fine.

◆ Preheat breakfast sandwich maker

1	English muffin, split in half	1
2	slices kosher pickle, cut crosswise	2
1	slice Gruyère cheese	1
2 to 3	slices deli corned beef	2 to 3
	Nonstick cooking spray	
1	large egg	1

1. Place one English muffin half, split side up, in bottom ring of sandwich maker. Top with pickles, cheese and beef.

2. Lower the cooking plate and top ring. Lightly spray the plate with cooking spray, then crack the egg into the ring. Pierce top of egg yolk with a toothpick or plastic fork. Place the other muffin half, split side down, on top of the egg.

3. Gently close the cover and cook for 4 to 5 minutes or until egg is cooked to your liking. Rotate cooking plate away from sandwich maker and lift rings. Use a plastic or nylon spatula to remove the sandwich. Serve immediately.

Variations

If you have leftover coleslaw, add 2 to 3 tbsp (30 to 45 mL) on top of the muffin in place of the pickles.

Edam or Gouda cheese would be a nice alternative to Gruyère here. Edam will also give the sandwich a nutty flavor, while Gouda will add more of a caramel flavor.

Breakfast Cheeseburger

This classic cheeseburger takes on a new twist with the addition of an egg, for a protein-packed power sandwich.

PREP TIME:
1 MINUTES

COOK TIME:
4 TO 5 MINUTES

Tip

The french-fried onions are the ones used on the traditional American Thanksgiving green bean dish.

◆ Preheat breakfast sandwich maker

1	4-inch (10 cm) burger bun, split in half	1
2½ oz	cooked beef patty (see box, page 68)	75 g
1	slice Cheddar cheese	1
	Nonstick cooking spray	
1	large egg	1
1 tbsp	french-fried onions (optional)	15 mL

1. Place bottom half of bun, split side up, in bottom ring of sandwich maker. Top with beef patty and cheese.

2. Lower the cooking plate and top ring. Lightly spray the plate with cooking spray, then crack the egg into the ring. Pierce top of egg yolk with a toothpick or plastic fork. Sprinkle with french-fried onions (if using). Place the other bun half, split side down, on top of the egg.

3. Gently close the cover and cook for 4 to 5 minutes or until an instant-read thermometer inserted in the center of the beef patty registers 165°F (74°C). Rotate cooking plate away from sandwich maker and lift rings. Use a plastic or nylon spatula to remove the burger. Serve immediately.

Burger Tips

If you're cooking your own homemade beef patties, shape the ground beef into rounds about 3½ inches (8.5 cm) in diameter and ½ inch (1 cm) thick. (I fill the top of a wide-mouth canning jar lid — it makes the perfect size patties.) You can season the patties with salt, pepper or any other seasonings you like before you cook them.

Cook and freeze your own beef patties ahead of time. Place waxed paper or foil between the patties so it is easier to remove single patties later. Frozen cooked patties can be stored in the freezer for up to 3 months.

You can also find frozen cooked beef patties in the freezer case at your local grocery store. They come in a range of sizes. Make sure to choose patties that weigh about 2½ oz (75 g) or less per patty, so that they will heat through in the sandwich maker.

You can add frozen patties directly to the breakfast sandwich maker, but if you find that they are not heating through in the specified time, try microwaving them on High for 40 to 50 seconds before adding them to the sandwich maker.

The Classic Cheeseburger

This cheeseburger is great for busy days around the house when everyone has different activities and wants to eat at separate times. With ready-made ingredients, everyone can have a quick and delicious meal.

PREP TIME:
2 MINUTES

COOK TIME:
4 TO 5 MINUTES

Tip

Have all of your ingredients ready to go. I keep a container in the refrigerator with the buns, beef patties, cheese and tomato slices. Then I leave a note on the fridge with the preparation instructions for the meal.

• Preheat breakfast sandwich maker

1	4-inch (10 cm) burger bun, split in half	1
2½ oz	cooked beef patty (see box, page 68)	75 g
1	slice Cheddar cheese	1
1	slice tomato	1
Pinch	salt (optional)	Pinch
Pinch	freshly ground black pepper (optional)	Pinch
	Ketchup (optional)	
	Mustard (optional)	

1. Place bottom half of bun, split side up, in bottom ring of sandwich maker. Top with beef patty, cheese and tomato. Season with salt and pepper (if using).

2. Lower the cooking plate and top ring. Place the other bun half, split side down, in top ring.

3. Gently close the cover and cook for 4 to 5 minutes or until an instant-read thermometer inserted in the center of the beef patty registers 165°F (74°C). Rotate cooking plate away from sandwich maker and lift rings. Use a plastic or nylon spatula to remove the burger.

4. If desired, lift the top bun and add ketchup and mustard to the burger. Serve immediately.

Blue Cheese Burger with Bacon

The pleasantly sharp taste of the blue cheese and the smoky flavor of the crunchy bacon make a delicious combination in this burger.

PREP TIME:

1 MINUTES

COOK TIME:

4 TO 5 MINUTES

Tip

You can also precook your bacon strips and have them ready to go. Alternatively, cooked bacon strips can be found alongside regular bacon products at the grocery store.

♦ Preheat breakfast sandwich maker

1	4-inch (10 cm) burger bun, split in half	1
2½ oz	cooked beef patty (see box, page 68)	75 g
2 tbsp	crumbled blue cheese	30 mL
2	slices bacon, cooked crisp	2

1. Place bottom half of bun, split side up, in bottom ring of sandwich maker. Top with beef patty and blue cheese. Break bacon into pieces that fit in the ring and add on top of the cheese.

2. Lower the cooking plate and top ring. Place the other bun half, split side down, in top ring.

3. Gently close the cover and cook for 4 to 5 minutes or until an instant-read thermometer inserted in the center of the beef patty registers 165°F (74°C). Rotate cooking plate away from sandwich maker and lift rings. Use a plastic or nylon spatula to remove the burger. Serve immediately.

Patty Melt

The traditional patty melt is a roadside diner staple in many areas. My version uses sourdough bread instead of the more traditional rye bread.

PREP TIME:

3 MINUTES

COOK TIME:

4 TO 5 MINUTES

Variations

If you like your onions more caramelized, cook them with the butter in a small skillet over low heat, stirring occasionally, until done to your liking.

Swiss cheese makes a nice substitution for the Cheddar cheese.

Omit the top slice of bread and serve the sandwich open-face.

◆ Preheat breakfast sandwich maker

2	slices sourdough bread, cut into 4-inch (10 cm) rounds	2
2½ oz	cooked beef patty (see box, page 68)	75 g
1	slice Cheddar cheese	1
Pinch	salt (optional)	Pinch
Pinch	freshly ground black pepper (optional)	Pinch
1 tbsp	butter	15 mL
⅓ cup	sliced onion	75 mL

1. Place one bread slice in bottom ring of sandwich maker. Top with beef patty and cheese. Season with salt and pepper (if using).

2. Lower the cooking plate and top ring. Add butter to the cooking plate and let it melt slightly. Add sliced onion. Place the other bread slice on top of the onion.

3. Gently close the cover and cook for 4 to 5 minutes or until an instant-read thermometer inserted in the center of the beef patty registers 165°F (74°C). Rotate cooking plate away from sandwich maker and lift rings. Use a plastic or nylon spatula to remove the sandwich. Serve immediately.

Pork Sandwiches

Pork Tenderloin and Apricot Sandwich

Simple yet elegant, pork tenderloin with a smear of sweet apricot preserves is a delightful breakfast treat.

PREP TIME:

1 MINUTE

COOK TIME:

4 TO 5 MINUTES

Tips

You can use up leftover pork tenderloin to make this yummy sandwich. I have also found nice round slices of cooked pork chop or tenderloin in the meat section of my local grocery store.

Any flavor of fruit preserves will work well in place of the apricot preserves.

◆ Preheat breakfast sandwich maker

2	slices sourdough bread, cut into 4-inch (10 cm) rounds	2
2 to 3	thin slices cooked pork tenderloin	2 to 3
1 tbsp	apricot preserves	15 mL
	Nonstick cooking spray	
1	large egg	1

1. Place one bread slice in bottom ring of sandwich maker. Top with pork and apricot preserves.

2. Lower the cooking plate and top ring. Lightly spray the plate with cooking spray, then crack the egg into the ring. Pierce top of egg yolk with a toothpick or plastic fork. Place the other bread slice on top of the egg.

3. Gently close the cover and cook for 4 to 5 minutes or until egg is cooked to your liking. Rotate cooking plate away from sandwich maker and lift rings. Use a plastic or nylon spatula to remove the sandwich. Serve immediately.

Pulled Pork and Coleslaw Sandwich

If you have never tried a pulled pork sandwich with coleslaw on top, you are in for a treat. The tanginess of the coleslaw pairs wonderfully with the sweet and spicy barbecue flavor of the pulled pork.

PREP TIME:

1 MINUTE

COOK TIME:

4 TO 5 MINUTES

Tips

Pulled barbecued pork can be purchased in tubs or packages at the grocery store. There will be enough servings in the tub to make more sandwiches for busy days. Alternatively you can use leftovers from a roast (freeze individual portions for easy sandwich making) with a dollop of barbecue sauce to taste.

◆ Preheat breakfast sandwich maker

1	4-inch (10 cm) sandwich bun, split in half	1
2/3 cup	pulled barbecued pork	150 mL
2 tbsp	coleslaw	30 mL
	Nonstick cooking spray	
1	large egg	1

1. Place bottom half of bun, split side up, in bottom ring of sandwich maker. Top with pork and coleslaw.

2. Lower the cooking plate and top ring. Lightly spray the plate with cooking spray, then crack the egg into the ring. Pierce top of egg yolk with a toothpick or plastic fork. Place the other bun half, split side down, on top of the egg.

3. Gently close the cover and cook for 4 to 5 minutes or until egg is cooked to your liking. Rotate cooking plate away from sandwich maker and lift rings. Use a plastic or nylon spatula to remove the sandwich. Serve immediately.

Variations

Add a slice of your favorite cheese on top of the pork.

Pulled barbecued beef or chicken are wonderful alternatives to the pork.

Roast Pork and Swiss on Multigrain Bread

You won't have to go to a delicatessen to enjoy this great sandwich, but it will sure taste like you picked it up there.

Tips

If you have leftover pork roast on hand, use slices of that in place of the deli roast pork.

For a real New York deli experience and added flavor, use kosher pickles.

◆ Preheat breakfast sandwich maker

1 tbsp	Dijon mustard	15 mL
2	slices multigrain bread, cut into 4-inch (10 cm) rounds	2
1	slice Swiss cheese	1
2	slices pickle	2
2 to 3	slices deli roast pork	2 to 3
	Nonstick cooking spray	
1	large egg	1

1. Spread mustard on one side of each bread slice. Place one slice, spread side up, in bottom ring of sandwich maker. Top with cheese, pickles and pork.

2. Lower the cooking plate and top ring. Lightly spray the plate with cooking spray, then crack the egg into the ring. Pierce top of egg yolk with a toothpick or plastic fork. Place the other bread slice, spread side down, on top of the egg.

3. Gently close the cover and cook for 4 to 5 minutes or until egg is cooked to your liking. Rotate cooking plate away from sandwich maker and lift rings. Use a plastic or nylon spatula to remove the sandwich. Serve immediately.

Variation

Substitute hearty pumpernickel or rye bread slices.

Green Eggs and Ham Sandwich

Okay, the egg itself isn't green, but a little bit of whimsy is a great way to start the day.

PREP TIME:
3 MINUTES

COOK TIME:
4 TO 5 MINUTES

Tips

Want your kids to enjoy breakfast more? Try reading the Dr. Seuss classic *Green Eggs and Ham* to them while they are eating this sandwich.

You can use frozen chopped spinach instead of fresh. Cut off about a 2-inch (5 cm) cube of frozen spinach; defrost and squeeze the moisture out before adding it to the egg.

• Preheat breakfast sandwich maker

1	large egg	1
2/3 cup	chopped baby spinach	150 mL
1	English muffin, split in half	1
1	slice Cheddar cheese	1
1	slice cooked ham (about 1/4 inch/0.5 cm thick)	1
	Nonstick cooking spray	

1. In a small bowl, gently whisk egg. Stir in spinach. Set aside.

2. Place one muffin half, split side up, in bottom ring of sandwich maker. Top with cheese and ham.

3. Lower the cooking plate and top ring. Lightly spray the plate with cooking spray, then pour in the egg mixture. Place the other muffin half, split side down, on top of the egg.

4. Gently close the cover and cook for 4 to 5 minutes or until egg is cooked to your liking. Rotate cooking plate away from sandwich maker and lift rings. Use a plastic or nylon spatula to remove the sandwich. Serve immediately.

Ham and Gorgonzola Sandwich

This sandwich is a great make-ahead option to pack for lunch. I like to fire up my breakfast sandwich maker in the morning for a quick breakfast, then make this sandwich to pack and go.

Tip

For the bread, just choose your favorite artisan loaf. Any flavor will work well in this recipe.

Variation

Omit the egg and rosemary. Instead of adding the pecans in step 1, lightly spray the cooking plate with cooking spray, then add the pecans to the plate. Place the top bread slice on top of the pecans. Cook for 3 to 4 minutes or until sandwich is warmed through and pecans are lightly toasted.

◆ Preheat breakfast sandwich maker

2	slices artisan bread (see tip, at left), cut into 4-inch (10 cm) rounds	2
1	slice cooked ham (about $\frac{1}{4}$ inch/0.5 cm thick)	1
1	slice Gorgonzola cheese	1
2 tsp	chopped pecans	10 mL
	Nonstick cooking spray	
1	large egg	1
Pinch	fresh rosemary leaves (optional)	Pinch

1. Place one bread slice in bottom ring of sandwich maker. Top with ham and cheese. Sprinkle with pecans.

2. Lower the cooking plate and top ring. Lightly spray the plate with cooking spray, then crack the egg into the ring. Pierce top of egg yolk with a toothpick or plastic fork. Sprinkle with rosemary (if using). Place the other bread slice on top of the egg.

3. Gently close the cover and cook for 4 to 5 minutes or until egg is cooked to your liking. Rotate cooking plate away from sandwich maker and lift rings. Use a plastic or nylon spatula to remove the sandwich. Serve immediately.

Ham, Brie and Fig on French Bread

One of my all-time favorite snacks or appetizers is Brie and fig spread on crackers. You can now enjoy this delightful combination in sandwich form.

PREP TIME:

2 MINUTES

COOK TIME:

4 TO 5 MINUTES

Tip

You can find Brie in small, individually packed wedges at most grocery stores. These make for easy preparation for this sandwich and are also great to take along as an afternoon snack.

Variation

Use Havarti cheese in place of the Brie.

◆ Preheat breakfast sandwich maker

2	slices French bread, cut into 4-inch (10 cm) rounds if necessary	2
2 to 3	sliced deli ham	2 to 3
1 to 2	slices Brie cheese	1 to 2
1 tbsp	fig spread	15 mL
	Nonstick cooking spray	
1	large egg	1

1. Place one bread slice in bottom ring of sandwich maker. Top with ham, cheese and fig spread.

2. Lower the cooking plate and top ring. Lightly spray the plate with cooking spray, then crack the egg into the ring. Pierce top of egg yolk with a toothpick or plastic fork. Place the other bread slice on top of the egg.

3. Gently close the cover and cook for 4 to 5 minutes or until egg is cooked to your liking. Rotate cooking plate away from sandwich maker and lift rings. Use a plastic or nylon spatula to remove the sandwich. Serve immediately.

Ham and Cranberry Relish on Sweet Potato Pancakes

This combination of flavors reminds me of a festive holiday dinner. Sweet potato pancakes make a great sandwich bun.

PREP TIME:
1 MINUTE

COOK TIME:
4 TO 5 MINUTES

Tips

Cranberry relish is a tradition in many U.S. households for the Thanksgiving meal, but jellied cranberry sauce will also work well. Alternatively, you could add dried or fresh cranberries to your sandwich.

Save leftovers from a large holiday meal in individual portions for easy sandwich making.

♦ Preheat breakfast sandwich maker

2	frozen cooked sweet potato pancakes	2
1	slice Monterey Jack cheese	1
1	slice cooked ham (about ¼ inch/0.5 cm thick)	1
2 tsp	cranberry relish	10 mL
	Nonstick cooking spray	
1	large egg	1

1. Place a pancake in bottom ring of sandwich maker. Top with cheese, ham and cranberry relish.

2. Lower the cooking plate and top ring. Lightly spray the plate with cooking spray, then crack the egg into the ring. Pierce top of egg yolk with a toothpick or plastic fork. Place the other pancake on top of the egg.

3. Gently close the cover and cook for 4 to 5 minutes or until egg is cooked to your liking. Rotate cooking plate away from sandwich maker and lift rings. Use a plastic or nylon spatula to remove the sandwich. Serve immediately.

Variations

Use Canadian bacon or cooked pork in place of the ham.

Replace the pancakes with bread slices or an English muffin and add 1½ tbsp (22 mL) leftover mashed sweet potato to the sandwich before the cranberry relish.

Prosciutto and Artichokes on Brioche

Almost like warm spinach artichoke dip, but in a breakfast sandwich to go.

PREP TIME:
2 MINUTES

COOK TIME:
4 TO 5 MINUTES

Tip

The artichokes are packed in a flavorful oil. Drizzle a little on the split sides of the bun before you add the other ingredients.

- Preheat breakfast sandwich maker

1	4-inch (10 cm) brioche bun, split in half	1
½ cup	baby spinach, divided	125 mL
2 tbsp	diced drained oil-packed or marinated artichoke hearts	30 mL
1	slice fontina cheese	1
2 to 3	thin slices prosciutto	2 to 3
	Nonstick cooking spray	
1	large egg	1

1. Place bottom half of bun, split side up, in bottom ring of sandwich maker. Add half of the spinach. Top with artichokes, cheese and prosciutto.

2. Lower the cooking plate and top ring. Lightly spray the plate with cooking spray, then crack the egg into the ring. Pierce top of egg yolk with a toothpick or plastic fork. Top with the remaining spinach. Place the other bun half, split side down, on top of spinach.

3. Gently close the cover and cook for 4 to 5 minutes or until egg is cooked to your liking. Rotate cooking plate away from sandwich maker and lift rings. Use a plastic or nylon spatula to remove the sandwich. Serve immediately.

Salami and Sharp Cheddar on Caraway Bread

This sandwich reminds me of summer days playing outside at my grandparents' home. When we dashed into the house, my grandmother always had sliced salami, cheese and bread or crackers ready for us to make up into a quick snack.

PREP TIME:

2 MINUTES

COOK TIME:

4 TO 5 MINUTES

Tip

Use any type of salami that happens to pique your interest at the grocery store. There are so many varieties to try, you may never tire of this sandwich. Salami flavored with peppercorns, fennel or garlic works particularly well.

- ◆ Preheat breakfast sandwich maker

2 tsp	coarse mustard (optional)	10 mL
2	slices caraway bread, cut into 4-inch (10 cm) rounds	2
1	slice sharp (old) Cheddar cheese	1
2	slices salami	2
	Nonstick cooking spray	
1	large egg	1
1	ring red onion	1

1. If desired, spread mustard on one side of each bread slice. Place one slice, spread side up, in bottom ring of sandwich maker. Top with cheese and salami.

2. Lower the cooking plate and top ring. Lightly spray the plate with cooking spray, then crack the egg into the ring. Pierce top of egg yolk with a toothpick or plastic fork. Top with onion ring. Place the other bread slice, spread side down, on top of the egg.

3. Gently close the cover and cook for 4 to 5 minutes or until egg is cooked to your liking. Rotate cooking plate away from sandwich maker and lift rings. Use a plastic or nylon spatula to remove the sandwich. Serve immediately.

Zesty Bologna on Rye

The combination of onion relish and bologna will remind you of eating outside at a ball game or from your favorite street vendor on a warm summer day.

PREP TIME:
2 MINUTES

COOK TIME:
4 TO 5 MINUTES

Tip

Any brand of onion relish will work well for this sandwich, or, to make your own sweet onion relish, melt 2 tbsp (30 mL) butter over low heat. Add 1 chopped large onion and cook, stirring occasionally, for 20 to 30 minutes or until softened and golden brown. Add 1 tbsp (15 mL) packed brown sugar and 2 tsp (10 mL) cider vinegar; cook, stirring, until liquid has evaporated. You will have slightly less than ½ cup (125 mL) of onion relish. Store in an airtight container in the refrigerator for up to 3 weeks.

◆ Preheat breakfast sandwich maker

1½ tbsp	coarse mustard	22 mL
1 tbsp	onion relish	15 mL
2	slices rye bread, cut into 4-inch (10 cm) rounds	2
1	slice bologna	1
	Nonstick cooking spray	
1	large egg	1

1. Spread mustard and onion relish on one side of each bread slice. Place one slice, spread side up, in bottom ring of sandwich maker. Top with bologna.

2. Lower the cooking plate and top ring. Lightly spray the plate with cooking spray, then crack the egg into the ring. Pierce top of egg yolk with a toothpick or plastic fork. Place the other bread slice, spread side down, on top of the egg.

3. Gently close the cover and cook for 4 to 5 minutes or until egg is cooked to your liking. Rotate cooking plate away from sandwich maker and lift rings. Use a plastic or nylon spatula to remove the sandwich. Serve immediately.

Variations

Pumpernickel bread is a nice full-flavor alternative to the rye bread.

Use Italian mortadella in place of the bologna, or try a German style of bologna, which will give your sandwich a garlicky flavor.

Pancetta and Smoked Gouda on Sourdough

The flavors of pancetta, Gouda and green olives in this sandwich meld into a smoky, salty, rich extravaganza.

PREP TIME:

2 MINUTES

COOK TIME:

4 TO 5 MINUTES

Tips

Cook pancetta as you would cook bacon. A small skillet makes it easier to get just the right doneness. To make sandwich preparation faster, cook a larger amount of pancetta in advance. Cooked pancetta can be stored in the refrigerator for up to 3 weeks.

If you are purchasing pancetta from the deli, ask them to cut it into 1-inch (2.5 cm) thick slices. This will make it easier to chop into nice size cubes for cooking.

• Preheat breakfast sandwich maker

2	slices sourdough bread, cut into 4-inch (10 cm) rounds	2
1	slice smoked Gouda cheese	1
3 tbsp	cooked chopped pancetta (see tips, at left)	45 mL
1 tbsp	chopped green olives	15 mL
	Nonstick cooking spray	
1	large egg	1

1. Place one bread slice in bottom ring of sandwich maker. Top with cheese, pancetta and olives.

2. Lower the cooking plate and top ring. Lightly spray the plate with cooking spray, then crack the egg into the ring. Pierce top of egg yolk with a toothpick or plastic fork. Place the other bread slice on top of the egg.

3. Gently close the cover and cook for 4 to 5 minutes or until egg is cooked to your liking. Rotate cooking plate away from sandwich maker and lift rings. Use a plastic or nylon spatula to remove the sandwich. Serve immediately.

Variation

Substitute bacon for the pancetta and use regular Gouda instead of smoked. The smoky flavor of this version will be much less intense.

Peachy Canadian Bacon and Havarti Sandwich

The fresh, tangy flavor of peach preserves is a nice complement to the bacon and creamy Havarti in this sandwich.

PREP TIME:
1 MINUTE

COOK TIME:
4 TO 5 MINUTES

Tip

You may know Canadian bacon as back bacon, which is what it is called in many parts of the world. It is actually more similar to ham than to bacon, as it is much leaner and is cut from the loin. This type of bacon is fully cooked. If you want to use peameal bacon (cornmeal-crusted cured pork loin), you will need to cook it before adding it to the sandwich maker.

◆ Preheat breakfast sandwich maker

1½ tbsp	peach preserves	22 mL
1	English muffin, split in half	1
1	slice Havarti cheese	1
1	slice Canadian bacon	1
	Nonstick cooking spray	
1	large egg	1

1. Spread peach preserves on the split side of each muffin half. Place one half, spread side up, in bottom ring of sandwich maker. Top with cheese and bacon.

2. Lower the cooking plate and top ring. Lightly spray the plate with cooking spray, then crack the egg into the ring. Pierce top of egg yolk with a toothpick or plastic fork. Place the other muffin half, spread side down, on top of the egg.

3. Gently close the cover and cook for 4 to 5 minutes or until egg is cooked to your liking. Rotate cooking plate away from sandwich maker and lift rings. Use a plastic or nylon spatula to remove the sandwich. Serve immediately.

Variation

Instead of the peach preserves, use a spoonful from a 4-oz (113 mL) snack container or small can of peaches. Eat the remaining peaches on the side. The sandwich will be a little juicier, so make sure to have plenty of napkins on hand.

Bacon, Spinach and Blue Cheese Sandwich

The combination of bacon, spinach and blue cheese is wonderful on just about anything — sandwiches, salads, burgers . . . and breakfast sandwiches too!

PREP TIME:
2 MINUTES

COOK TIME:
4 TO 5 MINUTES

Tips

Containers of crumbled blue cheese make it easy to measure out just the right amount for a recipe.

Blue cheese stores well in the refrigerator for 3 to 4 weeks. Its flavor becomes stronger over time.

Use Gorgonzola for the blue cheese, for an earthy, robust taste and a creamy texture.

◆ Preheat breakfast sandwich maker

2 tsp	balsamic vinaigrette	10 mL
1	English muffin, split in half	1
3	baby spinach leaves	3
1 tbsp	crumbled blue cheese	15 mL
3	slices bacon, cooked crisp	3
	Nonstick cooking spray	
1	large egg	1
1	ring red onion	1

1. Drizzle vinaigrette on the split side of each muffin half. Place one half, split side up, in bottom ring of sandwich maker. Top with spinach and cheese. Break bacon into pieces that fit in the ring and add on top of the cheese.

2. Lower the cooking plate and top ring. Lightly spray the plate with cooking spray, then crack the egg into the ring. Pierce top of egg yolk with a toothpick or plastic fork. Top with onion ring. Place the other muffin half, split side down, on top of the egg.

3. Gently close the cover and cook for 4 to 5 minutes or until egg is cooked to your liking. Rotate cooking plate away from sandwich maker and lift rings. Use a plastic or nylon spatula to remove the sandwich. Serve immediately.

Apple, Sausage and Cheddar Croissant

The unique combination of tart apples, sausage and cheese adds a robust taste to this croissant sandwich.

PREP TIME:

2 MINUTES

COOK TIME:

4 TO 5 MINUTES

Tips

Tart green apples, such as a Granny Smith or Fuji, complement the sausage and sharp Cheddar flavors of this light croissant.

Serve the remainder of the apple alongside your sandwich or pack it in an airtight container for a midday snack.

◆ Preheat breakfast sandwich maker

1	small croissant, split in half	1
1	frozen cooked pork sausage patty	1
¼	tart green apple, thinly sliced	¼
1 tbsp	packed brown sugar	15 mL
	Nonstick cooking spray	
1	large egg	1
2 tbsp	shredded sharp (old) Cheddar cheese	30 mL

1. Place bottom half of croissant, split side up, in bottom ring of sandwich maker. Top with sausage and apple slices. Sprinkle apples with brown sugar.

2. Lower the cooking plate and top ring. Lightly spray the plate with cooking spray, then crack the egg into the ring. Pierce top of egg yolk with a toothpick or plastic fork. Sprinkle cheese on top of the egg. Place the other croissant half, split side down, on top of the cheese.

3. Gently close the cover and cook for 4 to 5 minutes or until egg is cooked to your liking. Rotate cooking plate away from sandwich maker and lift rings. Use a plastic or nylon spatula to remove the sandwich. Serve immediately.

Variation

Caramelize the apple slices: Place the apple slices, brown sugar and 1 tsp (5 mL) butter in a small bowl. Cover and microwave on High for 5 minutes. Pour on top of sausage patty in sandwich maker.

Summer Sausage and Pepper Jack Sandwich

The robust flavor of summer sausage works well with the kick of pepper Jack cheese on a hot summer day.

PREP TIME:

2 MINUTES

COOK TIME:

4 TO 5 MINUTES

Tip

Summer sausage is often made with pork, but you can also find beef summer sausage or a combination of both beef and pork. Any type will taste great in this sandwich.

- Preheat breakfast sandwich maker

2 tsp	mayonnaise (optional)	10 mL
2	slices whole wheat bread, cut into 4-inch (10 cm) rounds	2
1	slice pepper Jack cheese	1
2	slices cooked summer sausage	2
	Nonstick cooking spray	
1	large egg	1

1. If desired, spread mayonnaise on one side of each bread slice. Place one slice, spread side up, in bottom ring of sandwich maker. Top with cheese and sausage.

2. Lower the cooking plate and top ring. Lightly spray the plate with cooking spray, then crack the egg into the ring. Pierce top of egg yolk with a toothpick or plastic fork. Place the other bread slice, spread side down, on top of the egg.

3. Gently close the cover and cook for 4 to 5 minutes or until egg is cooked to your liking. Rotate cooking plate away from sandwich maker and lift rings. Use a plastic or nylon spatula to remove the sandwich. Serve immediately.

Variation

For a milder, less peppery sandwich, use Monterey Jack cheese.

Spinach and Parmesan on a Sausage Crust

A sausage patty stands in for the bread in this easy open-face sandwich, perfect for mornings when you'd just as soon omit bread from your meal.

PREP TIME:
2 MINUTES

COOK TIME:
4 TO 5 MINUTES

Tips

There are many varieties of cooked pork sausage patties. Try patties flavored with maple syrup, herbs or spices to add variety to your breakfast sandwiches.

You can assemble the sausage, spinach and cheese before placing the sausage in the bottom ring. Use a fork to lower the patty into the ring so you don't lose the other ingredients.

♦ Preheat breakfast sandwich maker

1	frozen cooked pork sausage patty	1
½ cup	baby spinach	125 mL
2 tbsp	freshly grated Parmesan cheese	30 mL
	Nonstick cooking spray	
1	large egg	1
Pinch	ground nutmeg (optional)	Pinch

1. Place sausage in bottom ring of sandwich maker. Top with spinach and cheese.

2. Lower the cooking plate and top ring. Lightly spray the plate with cooking spray, then crack the egg into the ring. Pierce top of egg yolk with a toothpick or plastic fork. Sprinkle with nutmeg, if using.

3. Gently close the cover and cook for 4 to 5 minutes or until egg is cooked to your liking. Rotate cooking plate away from sandwich maker and lift rings. Use a plastic or nylon spatula to remove the quiche. Serve immediately.

Chicken and Turkey Sandwiches

◇◇◇◇◇◇◇◇◇◇◇◇◇◇◇◇◇◇◇◇◇◇◇◇◇◇◇◇◇◇◇◇◇◇◇◇◇

Chicken and Monterey Jack on Egg Bread

This is a version of my absolute favorite grade-school lunch. My mom always used chunks of her leftover Sunday chicken dinner, which made my sandwich taste like real home cooking.

PREP TIME:

3 MINUTES

COOK TIME:

4 TO 5 MINUTES

Tip

Cutting the chicken into bite-size chunks makes this sandwich easier to eat.

You can use dark or white meat, or a combination of both.

If you are packing this sandwich for lunch, make sure you have an insulated cooler or can refrigerate it. It should not be left unrefrigerated for any length of time.

Plain yogurt is a nice substitute for the mayonnaise in this sandwich.

◆ Preheat breakfast sandwich maker

2 tsp	mayonnaise	10 mL
2	slices egg bread, cut into 4-inch (10 cm) rounds	2
1	slice Monterey Jack cheese	1
¼ cup	chopped leftover roasted chicken	60 mL
	Nonstick cooking spray	
1	large egg	1

1. Spread mayonnaise on one side of each bread slice. Place one slice, spread side up, in bottom ring of sandwich maker. Top with cheese and chicken.

2. Lower the cooking plate and top ring. Lightly spray the plate with cooking spray, then crack the egg into the ring. Pierce top of egg yolk with a toothpick or plastic fork. Place the other bread slice, spread side down, on top of the egg.

3. Gently close the cover and cook for 4 to 5 minutes or until egg is cooked to your liking. Rotate cooking plate away from sandwich maker and lift rings. Use a plastic or nylon spatula to remove the sandwich. Serve immediately.

Honey Dijon Chicken Sandwich

The sharp, tangy flavors of Romano cheese make a nice complement to the honey Dijon and roasted chicken.

PREP TIME:

2 MINUTES

COOK TIME:

4 TO 5 MINUTES

Tips

Romano cheese can be made with either sheep's or cow's milk. The Italian version is made with sheep's milk and is called Pecorino Romano. Many American versions are made with cow's milk. Either type will taste great in this sandwich.

Deli roasted chicken slices, leftover chicken or cooked chicken breast are all good options to use in this recipe. I usually just use what I have on hand.

♦ Preheat breakfast sandwich maker

1 tbsp	honey Dijon mustard	15 mL
1	English muffin, split in half	1
1	slice Romano cheese	1
2 to 3	slices roasted chicken (see tip, at left)	2 to 3
	Nonstick cooking spray	
1	large egg	1

1. Spread honey mustard on split sides of English muffin. Place one muffin half, spread side up, in bottom ring of sandwich maker. Top with cheese and chicken.

2. Lower the cooking plate and top ring. Lightly spray the plate with cooking spray, then crack the egg into the ring. Pierce top of egg yolk with a toothpick or plastic fork. Place the other muffin half, spread side down, on top of the egg.

3. Gently close the cover and cook for 4 to 5 minutes or until egg is cooked to your liking. Rotate cooking plate away from sandwich maker and lift rings. Use a plastic or nylon spatula to remove the sandwich. Serve immediately.

Creamy Alfredo Chicken and Asparagus on Ciabatta

Alfredo sauce, typically used in pasta dishes, also makes a creamy, flavorful addition to the asparagus and chicken in this sandwich.

PREP TIME:
2 MINUTES

COOK TIME:
4 TO 5 MINUTES

Tip

Plan your evening meal in advance and use the leftover frozen asparagus as a side dish or add it to your favorite recipe. Alternatively, use just what you need for this recipe, reseal the package and use the remaining asparagus at a later time.

◆ Preheat breakfast sandwich maker

1	mini ciabatta roll (about 4 inches/10 cm in diameter), split in half	1
2 to 3	slices cooked chicken breast	2 to 3
3 tbsp	frozen cut asparagus spears	45 mL
1 tbsp	Alfredo sauce	15 mL
	Nonstick cooking spray	
1	large egg	1

1. Place bottom half of roll, cut side up, in bottom ring of sandwich maker. Top with chicken and asparagus. Drizzle with Alfredo sauce.

2. Lower the cooking plate and top ring. Lightly spray the plate with cooking spray, then crack the egg into the ring. Pierce top of egg yolk with a toothpick or plastic fork. Place the other roll half, cut side down, on top of the egg.

3. Gently close the cover and cook for 4 to 5 minutes or until egg is cooked to your liking. Rotate cooking plate away from sandwich maker and lift rings. Use a plastic or nylon spatula to remove the sandwich. Serve immediately.

Variation

Use just the bottom half of the ciabatta roll, for an open-face sandwich. Increase the Alfredo sauce to 2 tbsp (30 mL) and, instead of drizzling it over the chicken and asparagus in step 1, heat it briefly in the microwave while the sandwich is cooking. After removing the sandwich from the sandwich maker, drizzle the Alfredo sauce over top. This version looks and tastes a little more decadent.

Chicken and Artichoke Pesto on Focaccia

Tangy citrus and artichoke pesto make this chicken sandwich a Mediterranean treat. Top it with sprouts and you have a really delicious meal.

PREP TIME:
3 MINUTES

COOK TIME:
4 TO 5 MINUTES

Tips

Artichoke lemon pesto can be purchased in small jars at many grocery stores and specialty shops. You can also make it from scratch, if you have a recipe you love.

If you prefer crisper sprouts, add them after your sandwich is cooked instead. That way, you can also add a lot more of them if you love sprouts.

◆ Preheat breakfast sandwich maker

1½ tbsp	artichoke lemon pesto spread	22 mL
1	4-inch (10 cm) round piece of focaccia	1
2 to 3	slices deli roasted chicken	2 to 3
	Nonstick cooking spray	
1	large egg	1
	Mung bean sprouts	

1. Spread pesto on one side of focaccia. Place focaccia, spread side up, in bottom ring of sandwich maker. Top with chicken.

2. Lower the cooking plate and top ring. Lightly spray the plate with cooking spray, then crack the egg into the ring. Pierce top of egg yolk with a toothpick or plastic fork. Place sprouts on top of the egg.

3. Gently close the cover and cook for 4 to 5 minutes or until egg is cooked to your liking. Rotate cooking plate away from sandwich maker and lift rings. Use a plastic or nylon spatula to remove the sandwich. Serve immediately.

Variation

Alfalfa or broccoli sprouts also work nicely in place of the mung bean sprouts.

Chicken BLT

A bacon, lettuce and tomato sandwich is always a hit, and the chicken and egg in this version contribute more layers of protein.

PREP TIME:
2 MINUTES

COOK TIME:
4 TO 5 MINUTES

Tips

Adding the lettuce before cooking the sandwich means it is warm but less crunchy. If you prefer, you can add it after cooking. Turn the sandwich upside down, remove the bottom muffin, add the lettuce and replace the muffin. I don't recommend adding the lettuce to the top of the sandwich, because the muffin is too difficult to separate from the egg.

While iceberg is considered the traditional lettuce for a BLT, you may prefer to use spinach, arugula or mesclun, as they hold up better when warmed.

◆ Preheat breakfast sandwich maker

2 tsp	mayonnaise (optional)	10 mL
1	English muffin, split in half	1
	Iceberg lettuce leaves, torn to fit sandwich ring	
1	slice tomato	1
2	slices deli roasted chicken	2
2	slices bacon, cooked crisp	2
	Nonstick cooking spray	
1	large egg	1

1. If desired, spread mayonnaise on split sides of English muffin. Place one muffin half, split side up, in bottom ring of sandwich maker. Layer lettuce on top. Top with tomato and chicken. Break bacon into pieces that fit in the ring and place on top of the chicken.

2. Lower the cooking plate and top ring. Lightly spray the plate with cooking spray, then crack the egg into the ring. Pierce top of egg yolk with a toothpick or plastic fork. Place the other muffin half, split side down, on top of the egg.

3. Gently close the cover and cook for 4 to 5 minutes or until egg is cooked to your liking. Rotate cooking plate away from sandwich maker and lift rings. Use a plastic or nylon spatula to remove the sandwich. Serve immediately.

Leftover Turkey and Cranberry
Sauce on a Bagel (page 97)

**Smoked Salmon and Tapenade
on Flatbread (page 110)**

Provençal Avocado and
Garlic Aïoli Sandwich (page 147)

Pepperoni and Black Olive Pizza (page 159)

Cream Cheese, Jam and
Banana on Pancakes (page 166)

Marmalade, White Chocolate
and Coconut Sandwich (page 183)

Leftover Turkey and Cranberry Sauce on a Bagel

After a traditional holiday meal, we're always looking for ways to use up the leftovers. This tart and tasty breakfast sandwich is one delectable option.

PREP TIME:
2 MINUTES

COOK TIME:
4 TO 5 MINUTES

Tips

You may have to trim your bagel halves slightly around the edges to fit properly into the sandwich maker. Kitchen scissors work best for this task.

Jellied cranberry sauce is a tradition in many U.S. households for the traditional Thanksgiving meal, but any cranberry relish will also work well. You could also just add dried or fresh cranberries to your sandwich.

♦ Preheat breakfast sandwich maker

1 tbsp	spreadable cream cheese	15 mL
1	small thin bagel, split in half	1
1	slice jellied cranberry sauce	1
1	slice leftover turkey	1
	Nonstick cooking spray	
1	large egg	1

1. Spread cream cheese on split sides of bagel. Place one bagel half, spread side up, in bottom ring of sandwich maker. Top with cranberry sauce and turkey.

2. Lower the cooking plate and top ring. Lightly spray the plate with cooking spray, then crack the egg into the ring. Pierce top of egg yolk with a toothpick or plastic fork. Place the other bagel half, spread side down, on top of the egg.

3. Gently close the cover and cook for 4 to 5 minutes or until egg is cooked to your liking. Rotate cooking plate away from sandwich maker and lift rings. Use a plastic or nylon spatula to remove the sandwich. Serve immediately.

Variation

The sweet tartness of cranberries works well with horseradish. If you like horseradish, try spreading a little on top of the cream cheese.

Turkey and Butternut Squash Sandwich

Butternut squash is the perfect accompaniment to any fall meal. Its sweet, buttery taste and fibrous texture pairs well with the turkey in this delectable comfort food sandwich.

PREP TIME:
2 MINUTES

COOK TIME:
4 TO 5 MINUTES

Tips

This sandwich is very easy and practical if you have leftover turkey, squash and dinner rolls.

Use leftover mashed squash in this recipe. If you added brown sugar and butter when mashing it, it will still work wonderfully here.

Choose butternut squash that feels heavy for its size. The skin should be matte, not glossy. Glossiness usually indicates that the squash won't be as sweet because it has been harvested too early.

◆ Preheat breakfast sandwich maker

1	4-inch (10 cm) dinner roll, split in half	1
2 to 3	slices leftover turkey	2 to 3
3 tbsp	mashed butternut squash	45 mL
	Nonstick cooking spray	
1	large egg	1

1. Place bottom half of roll, split side up, in bottom ring of sandwich maker. Top with turkey and butternut squash.

2. Lower the cooking plate and top ring. Lightly spray the plate with cooking spray, then crack the egg into the ring. Pierce top of egg yolk with a toothpick or plastic fork. Place the other roll half, split side down, on top of the egg.

3. Gently close the cover and cook for 4 to 5 minutes or until egg is cooked to your liking. Rotate cooking plate away from sandwich maker and lift rings. Use a plastic or nylon spatula to remove the sandwich. Serve immediately.

Turkey, Havarti and Chia on Sourdough

Chia seeds have become a hit in health food circles, and this is an easy way to try them out. They give this sandwich a nice bit of crunchiness.

PREP TIME:
2 MINUTES

COOK TIME:
4 TO 5 MINUTES

Tips

Chia seeds were a prized food for the Aztec and Maya civilizations. You can use them in many ways: add them to smoothies and baked goods, or sprinkle them on yogurt and cereal.

Add chia seeds to fruit juice or water to make a popular Mexican drink called chia fresca. The seeds will expand to about 10 times their size and acquire a gelatinous texture. Chia fresca is a refreshing way to stay hydrated and will help you feel full.

◆ Preheat breakfast sandwich maker

2	slices sourdough bread, cut into 4-inch (10 cm) rounds	2
1	slice Havarti cheese	1
2 to 3	slices deli turkey	2 to 3
	Nonstick cooking spray	
1	large egg	1
2 tsp	chia seeds	10 mL

1. Place one bread slice in bottom ring of sandwich maker. Top with cheese and turkey.

2. Lower the cooking plate and top ring. Lightly spray the plate with cooking spray, then crack the egg into the ring. Pierce top of egg yolk with a toothpick or plastic fork. Sprinkle egg with chia seeds. Place the other bread slice on top of the egg.

3. Gently close the cover and cook for 4 to 5 minutes or until egg is cooked to your liking. Rotate cooking plate away from sandwich maker and lift rings. Use a plastic or nylon spatula to remove the sandwich. Serve immediately.

Turkey, Pepper Jack and Sun-Dried Tomato Sandwich

The robust flavors of sun-dried tomatoes and the peppers in the cheese add a gourmet feel to a simple turkey sandwich.

PREP TIME:
2 MINUTES

COOK TIME:
3 TO 4 MINUTES

Tip

You do not need to drain the sun-dried tomatoes thoroughly. A little bit of oil is a nice addition to the sandwich.

◆ Preheat breakfast sandwich maker

1	English muffin, split in half	1
2	oil-packed sun-dried tomatoes, drained and sliced	2
1	slice pepper Jack cheese	1
2	slices deli turkey	2
	Nonstick cooking spray	
1	large egg white	1

1. Place one English muffin half, split side up, in bottom ring of sandwich maker. Top with sun-dried tomatoes, cheese and turkey.

2. Lower the cooking plate and top ring. Lightly spray the plate with cooking spray, then add the egg white. Place the other English muffin, split side down, on top of the egg white.

3. Gently close the cover and cook for 3 to 4 minutes or until egg white is cooked through and no longer translucent. Rotate cooking plate away from sandwich maker and lift rings. Use a plastic or nylon spatula to remove the sandwich. Serve immediately.

Variation

If you don't have pepper Jack cheese on hand, use Swiss or Cheddar cheese and sprinkle it with hot pepper flakes.

Turkey Cobb Sandwich

Here you'll find many of the traditional flavors of a cobb salad, but on a quick and easy breakfast sandwich to eat on the go.

PREP TIME:

3 MINUTES

COOK TIME:

4 TO 5 MINUTES

Tip

If you have leftover roasted turkey on hand, this is a great way to use it up, in place of the sliced deli turkey.

◆ Preheat breakfast sandwich maker

2	slices multigrain bread, cut into 4-inch (10 cm) rounds	2
1	slice avocado	1
2	slices deli turkey	2
1 tbsp	crumbled blue cheese	15 mL
2	slices bacon, cooked crisp	2
	Nonstick cooking spray	
1	large egg	1

1. Place one bread slice in bottom ring of sandwich maker. Top with avocado, turkey and blue cheese. Break bacon into pieces that fit in the ring and add on top of the cheese.

2. Lower the cooking plate and top ring. Lightly spray the plate with cooking spray, then crack the egg into the ring. Pierce top of egg yolk with a toothpick or plastic fork. Place the other bread slice on top of the egg.

3. Gently close the cover and cook for 4 to 5 minutes or until egg is cooked to your liking. Rotate cooking plate away from sandwich maker and lift rings. Use a plastic or nylon spatula to remove the sandwich. Serve immediately.

Variation

A traditional cobb salad is also topped with tomato. You can add some chopped tomato here if you like. Because of the quantity of ingredients in the bottom ring, you should add the tomatoes on top of the egg.

Turkey Bacon and Provolone Sandwich

Turkey bacon usually has about 50% less fat than pork bacon, but still has lots of bacon taste and texture. Here, it combines with provolone and egg for a hearty morning meal.

PREP TIME:

2 MINUTES

COOK TIME:

4 TO 5 MINUTES

Tips

Use 2 egg whites, instead of the whole egg, if you are looking to reduce your cholesterol intake.

To make sandwich prep quicker and easier on busy mornings, cook up a package of turkey bacon in advance and store it in an airtight container in the refrigerator for up to 5 days, then just use what you need for your morning sandwich.

- ◆ Preheat breakfast sandwich maker

2	slices whole wheat bread, cut into 4-inch (10 cm) rounds	2
1	slice provolone cheese	1
3	slices turkey bacon, cooked crisp	3
	Nonstick cooking spray	
1	large egg	1

1. Place one bread slice in bottom ring of sandwich maker. Top with cheese. Break turkey bacon into pieces that fit in the ring and add on top of the cheese.

2. Lower the cooking plate and top ring. Lightly spray the plate with cooking spray, then crack the egg into the ring. Pierce top of egg yolk with a toothpick or plastic fork. Place the other bread slice on top of the egg.

3. Gently close the cover and cook for 4 to 5 minutes or until egg is cooked to your liking. Rotate cooking plate away from sandwich maker and lift rings. Use a plastic or nylon spatula to remove the sandwich. Serve immediately.

Turkey Sausage and Pepper Jack on Flatbread

Turkey sausage is a nice addition to any breakfast sandwich. You get all the sausage flavor and texture with about 65% less fat than pork sausages.

PREP TIME:

3 MINUTES

COOK TIME:

4 TO 5 MINUTES

Tip

You can find frozen cooked turkey sausage patties in the freezer section of your grocery store. Alternatively, you may find fresh cooked sausage patties in the meat section.

• Preheat breakfast sandwich maker

2	slices flatbread, cut into 4-inch (10 cm) rounds	2
1	frozen cooked turkey sausage patty	1
1	slice pepper Jack cheese	1
3	slices cucumber	3
	Nonstick cooking spray	
1	large egg	1

1. Place one flatbread slice in bottom ring of sandwich maker. Top with sausage, cheese and cucumber.

2. Lower the cooking plate and top ring. Lightly spray the plate with cooking spray, then crack the egg into the ring. Pierce top of egg yolk with a toothpick or plastic fork. Place the other flatbread slice on top of the egg.

3. Gently close the cover and cook for 4 to 5 minutes or until egg is cooked to your liking. Rotate cooking plate away from sandwich maker and lift rings. Use a plastic or nylon spatula to remove the sandwich. Serve immediately.

Variations

If you do not like the heat of pepper Jack cheese, plain Monterey Jack cheese works equally well in this sandwich.

Use pickle slices in place of the cucumbers. They will give an added tang that nicely complements the pepper Jack cheese and the spices in the sausage patty.

Fish and Seafood Sandwiches

◇◇◇◇◇◇◇◇◇◇◇◇◇◇◇◇◇◇◇◇◇◇◇◇◇◇◇◇◇◇◇◇◇◇◇◇◇◇◇

Kippers, Cucumber and Cream Cheese on Rye

Kippers (smoked herring) pair well with cucumbers and dill in this updated version of a longtime breakfast staple.

Tips

Kippers have seen a recent surge in popularity as people increasingly recognize the value of a sustainable fish that is both high in omega-3s and relatively inexpensive.

If you are watching your sodium consumption, keep in mind that kippers are high in sodium and pair them with lower-sodium ingredients.

Look for spreadable cream cheese with dill as an easy alternative to using dried dillweed.

* Preheat breakfast sandwich maker

1½ tbsp	spreadable cream cheese	22 mL
2	slices rye bread, cut into 4-inch (10 cm) rounds	2
Pinch	dried dillweed	Pinch
1	slice Monterey Jack cheese	1
½	can (4 oz/113 g) kippers, drained	½
1	slice cucumber	1
	Nonstick cooking spray	
1	large egg	1
1	slice tomato	1
Pinch	freshly ground black pepper (optional)	Pinch

1. Spread cream cheese on one side of each bread slice. Sprinkle cream cheese with dill. Place one bread slice, spread side up, in bottom ring of sandwich maker. Top with Monterey Jack, kippers and cucumber.

2. Lower the cooking plate and top ring. Lightly spray the plate with cooking spray, then crack the egg into the ring. Pierce top of egg yolk with a toothpick or plastic fork. Place tomato on top of the egg. Season with pepper (if using). Place the other bread slice, spread side down, on top of the tomato.

3. Gently close the cover and cook for 4 to 5 minutes or until egg is cooked to your liking. Rotate cooking plate away from sandwich maker and lift rings. Use a plastic or nylon spatula to remove the sandwich. Serve immediately.

Salmon, Caper and Egg White Sandwich

This version of an all-time classic has been slimmed down with an egg white, but still has rich flavor thanks to the salmon.

PREP TIME:
4 MINUTES

COOK TIME:
3 TO 4 MINUTES

Tip

Pink, chum or sockeye salmon will all work in this recipe, so just use your favorite.

Variations

Replace the salmon with 2 oz (60 g) lox — the cured and smoked belly portion of salmon. The resulting flavor will be saltier and smokier.

Replace the French bread with a bagel for a different flavor and texture.

♦ Preheat breakfast sandwich maker

1 tbsp	spreadable cream cheese	15 mL
2	slices French bread, cut into 4-inch (10 cm) rounds if necessary	2
½	can (5 oz/142 g) boneless skinless salmon, drained	½
1	slice tomato	1
	Nonstick cooking spray	
1	large egg white	1
1	ring red onion	1
1 tsp	drained capers	5 mL

1. Spread cream cheese on one side of each bread slice. Place one slice, spread side up, in bottom ring of sandwich maker. Top with salmon and tomato.

2. Lower the cooking plate and top ring. Lightly spray the plate with cooking spray, then add the egg white. Top with onion ring and capers. Place the other bread slice, spread side down, on top of the egg white.

3. Gently close the cover and cook for 3 to 4 minutes or until egg white is cooked through and no longer translucent. Rotate cooking plate away from sandwich maker and lift rings. Use a plastic or nylon spatula to remove the sandwich. Serve immediately.

Salmon, Ricotta and Mushrooms on Flatbread

When salmon, ricotta and mushrooms combine in this sandwich, you'll almost believe you are eating a yummy lasagna — but you prepared it in less than 10 minutes!

PREP TIME:
5 MINUTES

COOK TIME:
4 TO 5 MINUTES

Tips

Because salmon is so flavorful and rich, this sandwich will keep you satisfied for a long time. It's perfect for days when your schedule is packed and you don't know when your next meal will be.

Leftover salmon fillet can easily be used in place of the canned salmon. Use about ⅓ cup (75 mL) salmon chunks.

◆ Preheat breakfast sandwich maker

1	large egg	1
2 tbsp	chopped drained canned mushrooms	30 mL
Pinch	dried tarragon (optional)	Pinch
2	slices flatbread, cut into 4-inch (10 cm) rounds	2
2 tbsp	ricotta cheese	30 mL
½	can or pouch (5 oz/142 g) pink salmon, drained if necessary and broken into pieces	½
	Nonstick cooking spray	

1. In a small bowl, gently whisk egg. Stir in mushrooms and tarragon (if using). Set aside.

2. Place one flatbread slice in bottom ring of sandwich maker. Top with cheese and salmon.

3. Lower the cooking plate and top ring. Lightly spray the plate with cooking spray, then pour in the egg mixture. Place the other flatbread slice on top of the egg mixture.

4. Gently close the cover and cook for 4 to 5 minutes or until egg is cooked to your liking. Rotate cooking plate away from sandwich maker and lift rings. Use a plastic or nylon spatula to remove the sandwich. Serve immediately.

Variation

Chop a few spinach leaves and stir them into the egg mixture instead of, or in addition to, the mushrooms.

Smoked Salmon, Cream Cheese and Capers on a Bagel

The combination of smoked salmon, cream cheese, capers and a bagel is a timeless classic.

PREP TIME:
3 MINUTES

COOK TIME:
4 TO 5 MINUTES

Tips

You may have to trim your bagel halves slightly around the edges to fit properly into the sandwich maker. Kitchen scissors work best for this task.

Smoked salmon can be purchased in small pouches or cans that are just the right amount for your sandwich. But if you buy larger portions, smoked salmon also makes a great snack, served on crackers with cream cheese.

• Preheat breakfast sandwich maker

2 tbsp	spreadable cream cheese	30 mL
1	small thin bagel, split in half	1
2 oz	smoked salmon	60 g
	Nonstick cooking spray	
1	large egg	1
2 tsp	drained capers	10 mL

1. Spread cream cheese on split sides of bagel. Place one bagel half, spread side up, in bottom ring of sandwich maker. Top with salmon.

2. Lower the cooking plate and top ring. Lightly spray the plate with cooking spray, then crack the egg into the ring. Pierce top of egg yolk with a toothpick or plastic fork. Sprinkle with capers. Place the other bagel half, spread side down, on top of the egg.

3. Gently close the cover and cook for 4 to 5 minutes or until egg is cooked to your liking. Rotate cooking plate away from sandwich maker and lift rings. Use a plastic or nylon spatula to remove the sandwich. Serve immediately.

Variation

For a little extra flavor, use spreadable cream cheese with chives.

Smoked Salmon and Tapenade on Flatbread

The tasty combination of smoked salmon, black olive tapenade and flatbread will transport you to the Mediterranean with your first bite.

PREP TIME:		
3 MINUTES		

COOK TIME:		
3 TO 4 MINUTES		

Tip

If your flatbread does not fit well in the sandwich maker, trim the slices using kitchen shears. They do not have to be perfect rounds, but do need to lie flat inside the rings.

♦ Preheat breakfast sandwich maker

2	slices flatbread, cut into 4-inch (10 cm) rounds	2
1½ tbsp	black olive tapenade	22 mL
2 oz	smoked salmon	60 g
	Nonstick cooking spray	
1	large egg white	1
1	ring red onion (optional)	1

1. Spread tapenade on one side of one flatbread slice. Place flatbread slice, spread side up, in bottom ring of sandwich maker. Top with salmon.

2. Lower the cooking plate and top ring. Lightly spray the plate with cooking spray, then add the egg white. Top with onion ring (if using). Place the other flatbread slice on top.

3. Gently close the cover and cook for 3 to 4 minutes or until egg white is cooked through and no longer translucent. Rotate cooking plate away from sandwich maker and lift rings. Use a plastic or nylon spatula to remove the sandwich. Serve immediately.

Variation

For an extra protein punch, use 2 egg whites and increase the cooking time to 4 to 5 minutes.

Tuna Salad Sandwich

Tuna salad is a great standby for a quick sandwich anytime, and even novice chefs will find it easier to whip together.

PREP TIME:

6 MINUTES

COOK TIME:

4 TO 5 MINUTES

Tips

If you're too rushed to make your own tuna salad, premade versions are often available at the deli counter or in cans at the grocery store.

Mirepoix, a mix of chopped celery, onions and carrots, will also work nicely in the tuna salad. Use 2 tbsp (30 mL) mirepoix in place of the chopped celery and onion.

♦ Preheat breakfast sandwich maker

1	can (3 oz/85 g) water-packed tuna, drained	1
1 tbsp	chopped celery	15 mL
2 tsp	chopped onion	10 mL
1 tbsp	mayonnaise	15 mL
2	slices whole wheat bread, cut into 4-inch (10 cm) rounds	2
1	slice provolone cheese	1
	Nonstick cooking spray	
1	large egg	1

1. In a small bowl, combine tuna, celery, onion and mayonnaise.

2. Place one bread slice in bottom ring of sandwich maker. Top with cheese and tuna mixture.

3. Lower the cooking plate and top ring. Lightly spray the plate with cooking spray, then crack the egg into the ring. Pierce top of egg yolk with a toothpick or plastic fork. Place the other bread slice on top of the egg.

4. Gently close the cover and cook for 4 to 5 minutes or until egg is cooked to your liking. Rotate cooking plate away from sandwich maker and lift rings. Use a plastic or nylon spatula to remove the sandwich. Serve immediately.

Sweet and Spicy Tuna Melt

A bit of heat and a touch of honey offer a surprise twist on the usual tuna salad sandwich.

PREP TIME:

4 MINUTES

COOK TIME:

4 TO 5 MINUTES

Tip

Tuna also comes in pouches, which you may find easier to work with than cans.

◆ Preheat breakfast sandwich maker

1	can (3 oz/85 g) water-packed tuna, drained	1
1 tsp	chili powder	5 mL
1 tsp	liquid honey	5 mL
2	slices whole wheat bread, cut into 4-inch (10 cm) rounds	2
1	slice Swiss cheese	1
	Nonstick cooking spray	
1	large egg	1
Pinch	hot pepper flakes (optional)	Pinch

1. In a small bowl, combine tuna, chili powder and honey.

2. Place one bread slice in bottom ring of sandwich maker. Top with cheese and tuna mixture.

3. Lower the cooking plate and top ring. Lightly spray the plate with cooking spray, then crack the egg into the ring. Pierce top of egg yolk with a toothpick or plastic fork. Place the other bread slice on top of the egg.

4. Gently close the cover and cook for 4 to 5 minutes or until egg is cooked to your liking. Rotate cooking plate away from sandwich maker and lift rings. Use a plastic or nylon spatula to remove the sandwich. Serve immediately.

Variation

For a Chinese-inspired spin, add a pinch of ground ginger or a dash of sesame oil to the tuna mixture.

Tuna, Swiss and Tomato Sandwich

Tuna, Swiss and tomato combine to make a nice warm-weather sandwich that works well for breakfast or lunch.

PREP TIME:
3 MINUTES

COOK TIME:
4 TO 5 MINUTES

Tips

If you are packing this sandwich for lunch, make sure you have a cooler or refrigerator to store it in until you're ready to eat it.

Swiss cheese comes in regular or baby varieties. The most visible difference is the smaller holes in the baby Swiss. Baby Swiss is cured for a shorter time, giving it a milder, more buttery flavor, with just a hint of sweetness. It's a nice option for this sandwich.

♦ Preheat breakfast sandwich maker

1	English muffin, split in half	1
1	slice Swiss cheese	1
1	slice tomato	1
1	can (3 oz/85 g) water-packed tuna, drained	1
	Nonstick cooking spray	
1	large egg	1
Pinch	salt (optional)	Pinch
Pinch	freshly ground black pepper (optional)	Pinch

1. Place one English muffin half, split side up, in bottom ring of sandwich maker. Top with cheese, tomato and tuna.

2. Lower the cooking plate and top ring. Lightly spray the plate with cooking spray, then crack the egg into the ring. Pierce top of egg yolk with a toothpick or plastic fork. Season with salt and pepper (if using). Place the other muffin half, split side down, on top of the egg.

3. Gently close the cover and cook for 4 to 5 minutes or until egg is cooked to your liking. Rotate cooking plate away from sandwich maker and lift rings. Use a plastic or nylon spatula to remove the sandwich. Serve immediately.

Variation

Canned pink salmon works nicely in place of the tuna.

Baby Clam and Cream Cheese Sandwich

I love steamed clams with healthy dose of garlic, but they are not always readily available. Natural wood-smoked clams with a touch of garlic and cream cheese are a nice, easy alternative when you are craving clams.

PREP TIME:
3 MINUTES

COOK TIME:
4 TO 5 MINUTES

Tip

You can use canned clams that are not smoked, although you will lose that nice smoky flavor. Unsmoked canned clams come in larger, 10-oz (284 g) cans. Use ¼ cup (60 mL) drained clams. Store the remaining clams, with their liquid, in an airtight container in the refrigerator for up to 3 days. Leftover clams are easy to use in a pasta dish or in clam chowder.

◆ Preheat breakfast sandwich maker

2 tbsp	spreadable cream cheese	25 mL
Pinch	garlic powder	Pinch
2	slices French bread, cut into 4-inch (10 cm) rounds if necessary	2
½	can (3.75 oz/106 g) smoked baby clams, drained	½
	Nonstick cooking spray	
1	large egg	1

1. Spread cream cheese on one side of each bread slice. Sprinkle cream cheese with garlic powder. Place one bread slice, spread side up, in bottom ring of sandwich maker. Top with clams.

2. Lower the cooking plate and top ring. Lightly spray the plate with cooking spray, then crack the egg into the ring. Pierce top of egg yolk with a toothpick or plastic fork. Place the other bread slice, spread side down, on top of the egg.

3. Gently close the cover and cook for 4 to 5 minutes or until egg is cooked to your liking. Rotate cooking plate away from sandwich maker and lift rings. Use a plastic or nylon spatula to remove the sandwich. Serve immediately.

Crab Cake Benedict

A crab cake turns an already elegant breakfast dish into pure extravagance — wonderful for a lazy weekend morning.

PREP TIME:
2 MINUTES

COOK TIME:
4 TO 5 MINUTES

Tips

Packages of frozen cooked crab cakes usually have two cakes per package. Make two of these sandwiches for breakfast for two, or save the second crab cake for another meal.

For the hollandaise sauce, you can use a packaged sauce mix or premade sauce in a jar — or, if you have the time and a recipe you love, you can make it from scratch.

Leftover hollandaise sauce works wonderfully on top of asparagus and seafood fillets. If you plan ahead, you can use the sauce up within a few days.

◆ Preheat breakfast sandwich maker

½	English muffin	½
3 oz	frozen cooked crab cake	90 g
	Nonstick cooking spray	
1	large egg	1
3 tbsp	hollandaise sauce	45 mL

1. Place English muffin half, split side up, in bottom ring of sandwich maker. Top with crab cake.

2. Lower the cooking plate and top ring. Lightly spray the plate with cooking spray, then crack the egg into the ring. Pierce top of egg yolk with a toothpick or plastic fork.

3. Gently close the cover and cook for 4 to 5 minutes or until egg is cooked to your liking. Rotate cooking plate away from sandwich maker and lift rings. Use a plastic or nylon spatula to remove the sandwich.

4. Meanwhile, place the hollandaise sauce in a small bowl and microwave on High for 15 to 20 seconds or until warm. Drizzle over the egg. Serve immediately.

Deviled Crab Sandwich

Here, delicious deviled crab appears in a warm, crispy sandwich instead of topped with bread crumbs.

PREP TIME:
5 MINUTES

COOK TIME:
4 TO 5 MINUTES

Tips

Do not be tempted to use imitation crabmeat in this recipe; you will be disappointed by both the flavor and the consistency.

I like to chop onions for a few recipes in advance. They do not last as long once chopped, so just chop as much as you know you will use within a few days.

If you prefer less heat, omit the hot pepper sauce.

Store the remaining crabmeat, in its liquid, in an airtight container in the refrigerator for up to 3 days. Use it in one of your favorite recipes or in the sandwich on page 117.

◆ Preheat breakfast sandwich maker

½	can (6 oz/170 g) lump crabmeat, drained	½
1 tbsp	finely chopped onion	15 mL
1 tbsp	diced celery	15 mL
¼ tsp	dry mustard	1 mL
1 tbsp	mayonnaise	15 mL
1 tsp	Worcestershire sauce	5 mL
Dash	hot pepper sauce	Dash
1	4-inch (20 cm) long piece of baguette, split in half	1
	Nonstick cooking spray	
1	large egg	1

1. In a small bowl, combine crab, onion, celery, dry mustard, mayonnaise, Worcestershire sauce and hot pepper sauce.

2. Place bottom half of baguette, cut side up, in bottom ring of sandwich maker. Top with crab mixture.

3. Lower the cooking plate and top ring. Lightly spray the plate with cooking spray, then crack the egg into the ring. Pierce top of egg yolk with a toothpick or plastic fork. Place the other baguette half, cut side down, on top of the egg.

4. Gently close the cover and cook for 4 to 5 minutes or until egg is cooked to your liking. Rotate cooking plate away from sandwich maker and lift rings. Use a plastic or nylon spatula to remove the sandwich. Serve immediately.

Crab, Artichoke and Spinach Sandwich

The combination of crab, artichokes and spinach reminds me of a warm appetizer dip, so it's appropriately paired with French bread.

PREP TIME:
5 MINUTES

COOK TIME:
4 TO 5 MINUTES

Tip

Brush some of the oil from the packed artichokes onto the French bread before adding the other ingredients. Do not dip the pastry brush back into the artichoke jar, or you risk contaminating the remaining artichokes.

♦ Preheat breakfast sandwich maker

½	can (6 oz/170 g) lump crabmeat, drained	½
2 tbsp	chopped drained oil-packed or marinated artichoke hearts	30 mL
1	slice French bread, cut into a 4-inch (10 cm) round if necessary	1
5	baby spinach leaves, divided	5
	Nonstick cooking spray	
1	large egg	1

1. In a small bowl, combine crab and artichokes.

2. Place bread slice in bottom ring of sandwich maker. Layer 3 spinach leaves on top. Top with crab mixture.

3. Lower the cooking plate and top ring. Lightly spray the plate with cooking spray, then crack the egg into the ring. Pierce top of egg yolk with a toothpick or plastic fork. Top with the remaining spinach leaves.

4. Gently close the cover and cook for 4 to 5 minutes or until egg is cooked to your liking. Rotate cooking plate away from sandwich maker and lift rings. Use a plastic or nylon spatula to remove the sandwich. Serve immediately.

Variation

Lighten up this sandwich by using 2 egg whites instead of the egg.

Shrimp Scampi Sandwich

Shrimp scampi stars in a multitude of pasta dishes, and is just as wonderful in a delicious egg white sandwich.

PREP TIME:
5 MINUTES

COOK TIME:
3 TO 4 MINUTES

Tip

If you have leftover shrimp scampi, use about ¼ cup (60 mL) instead of making it from scratch.

• Preheat breakfast sandwich maker

½	can (4 oz/113 g) small or medium shrimp, drained	½
1	green onion, thinly sliced	1
1 tsp	dried parsley	5 mL
Pinch	garlic powder	Pinch
1 tbsp	butter, melted	15 mL
1	4-inch (10 cm) crusty sandwich bun, split in half	1
1	wedge lemon (optional)	1
	Nonstick cooking spray	
1	large egg white	1

1. In a small bowl, gently combine shrimp, green onion, parsley, garlic powder and butter.

2. Place bottom half of bun in bottom ring of sandwich maker. Top with shrimp mixture. If desired, squeeze lemon juice over top.

3. Lower the cooking plate and top ring. Lightly spray the plate with cooking spray, then add the egg white. Place the other bun half on top of the egg white.

4. Gently close the cover and cook for 3 to 4 minutes or until egg white is cooked through and no longer translucent. Rotate cooking plate away from sandwich maker and lift rings. Use a plastic or nylon spatula to remove the sandwich. Serve immediately.

Variation

Freshly grated Parmesan cheese is a nice addition to this sandwich. Sprinkle it on the egg before adding the top half of the bun.

Shrimp, Bacon and Swiss on Sourdough

I never really thought of pairing bacon with shrimp until I enjoyed a fantastic shrimp chowder with bacon and chives sprinkled on top. The combination is just as scrumptious in this sandwich.

PREP TIME:
3 MINUTES

COOK TIME:
3 TO 4 MINUTES

Tips

Add the leftover shrimp to canned cream of potato soup for a warm and hearty meal. Top it with some diced cooked bacon and chives.

Variations

Provolone cheese is a smoother-tasting alternative to the Swiss.

To give this sandwich a bit of a kick, add a dollop of prepared horseradish on top of the egg before adding the top bread slice.

• Preheat breakfast sandwich maker

2	slices sourdough bread, cut into 4-inch (10 cm) rounds	2
1	slice Swiss cheese	1
½	can (4 oz/113 g) small or medium shrimp, drained	½
2	slices bacon, cooked crisp	2
	Nonstick cooking spray	
1	large egg white	1
1 tsp	snipped fresh chives	5 mL
Pinch	salt (optional)	Pinch
Pinch	freshly ground black pepper (optional)	Pinch

1. Place one bread slice in bottom ring of sandwich maker. Top with cheese and shrimp. Break bacon into pieces that fit in the ring and add on top of the shrimp.

2. Lower the cooking plate and top ring. Lightly spray the plate with cooking spray, then add the egg white. Sprinkle with chives and season with salt and pepper (if using). Place the other bread slice on top of the egg white.

3. Gently close the cover and cook for 3 to 4 minutes or until egg white is cooked through and no longer translucent. Rotate cooking plate away from sandwich maker and lift rings. Use a plastic or nylon spatula to remove the sandwich. Serve immediately.

Gourmet Meals for One or Two

◇◇◇◇◇◇◇◇◇◇◇◇◇◇◇◇◇◇◇◇◇◇◇◇◇◇◇◇◇◇◇◇

Beef Wellington Sandwich

A quick alternative to an elegant beef Wellington, this sandwich uses leftover steak or beef tenderloin for your next-day feast.

PREP TIME:
10 MINUTES

COOK TIME:
4 TO 5 MINUTES

Tip

The mushroom mixture is really a treat, and the smell when you are sautéing it will make you hungry for more. I always make at least double the recipe, so it's ready for future sandwiches. Store it in an airtight container in the refrigerator for up to 3 days. Before using, reheat it in the microwave on High for 15 seconds or until the mixture is soft and spreadable.

◆ Preheat breakfast sandwich maker

1 tsp	butter	5 mL
3 tbsp	diced mushrooms	45 mL
1 tbsp	diced shallots	15 mL
Pinch	dried thyme	Pinch
1	large egg	1
½ tsp	dry mustard	2 mL
2	slices French bread, cut into 4-inch (10 cm) rounds if necessary	2
2 to 3	slices cooked prime beef steak or beef tenderloin	2 to 3
	Nonstick cooking spray	

1. In a small pan, melt butter over medium heat. Add mushrooms, shallots and thyme; cook, stirring, for about 3 minutes or until the moisture released from the mushrooms has evaporated. Remove from heat and set aside.

2. In a small bowl, whisk together egg and mustard.

3. Spread mushroom mixture on one side of each bread slice. Place one slice, spread side up, in bottom ring of sandwich maker. Top with beef slices.

4. Lower the cooking plate and top ring. Lightly spray the plate with cooking spray, then pour in the egg mixture. Place the other bread slice, spread side down, on top of the egg.

5. Gently close the cover and cook for 4 to 5 minutes or until egg is cooked to your liking. Rotate cooking plate away from sandwich maker and lift rings. Use a plastic or nylon spatula to remove the sandwich. Serve immediately.

Roast Beef and Butternut Squash on a Kaiser

Butternut squash has a sweet, buttery taste and an abundance of nutrients. Pair it with roast beef and a mini omelet, and you have a filling, energy-packed sandwich.

PREP TIME:
5 MINUTES

COOK TIME:
4 TO 5 MINUTES

Tips

If you find it easier (depending on the consistency of your mashed squash), you can spread the squash over the bottom half of the roll before placing the roll in the sandwich maker.

When you cook butternut squash, save some for your sandwiches. Cooked squash will keep for about 3 days in the refrigerator when sealed in an airtight container.

◆ Preheat breakfast sandwich maker

1	large egg	1
2 tsp	chopped green bell pepper	10 mL
2 tsp	chopped onion	10 mL
Pinch	salt (optional)	Pinch
Pinch	freshly ground black pepper (optional)	Pinch
1	4-inch (10 cm) Kaiser roll, split in half	1
3 tbsp	mashed cooked butternut squash	45 mL
3	thin slices deli roast beef	3
	Nonstick cooking spray	

1. In a small bowl, gently whisk egg. Stir in green pepper and onion. Season with salt and pepper (if using). Set aside.

2. Place bottom half of roll, split side up, in bottom ring of sandwich maker. Top with squash and roast beef.

3. Lower the cooking plate and top ring. Lightly spray the plate with cooking spray, then pour in the egg mixture. Place the other roll half, split side down, on top of the egg.

4. Gently close the cover and cook for 4 to 5 minutes or until egg is cooked to your liking. Rotate cooking plate away from sandwich maker and lift rings. Use a plastic or nylon spatula to remove the sandwich. Serve immediately.

Asian Burger on a Ramen Noodle Bun

The ramen noodle bun adds a unique twist to this spicy Asian burger. You may even find that you have a new favorite type of sandwich bun in your kitchen arsenal.

Tip

Prepare the ramen noodle buns ahead of time so you can make this sandwich quickly.

Variation

Use just one ramen noodle bun on the bottom of the sandwich and save the other one for later.

♦ Preheat breakfast sandwich maker

	Nonstick cooking spray	
2	Ramen Noodle Buns (see recipe, opposite)	2
1	slice Gouda cheese	1
2½ oz	cooked beef patty (see box, page 68)	75 g
1 tbsp	ketchup	15 mL
1½ tsp	Thai chile sauce (such as Sriracha)	7 mL
Dash	soy sauce (optional)	Dash
2 tsp	sliced green onion	10 mL
1	large egg	1

1. Lightly spray bottom plate of sandwich maker with cooking spray. Place one bun in bottom ring of sandwich maker. Top with cheese, beef patty, ketchup, chile sauce, soy sauce (if using) and green onion.

2. Lower the cooking plate and top ring. Lightly spray the plate with cooking spray, then crack the egg into the ring. Pierce top of egg yolk with a toothpick or plastic fork. Place the other bun on top of the egg.

3. Gently close the cover and cook for 4 to 5 minutes or until egg is cooked to your liking. Rotate cooking plate away from sandwich maker and lift rings. Use a plastic or nylon spatula to remove the sandwich. Serve immediately.

Ramen Noodle Buns

What student doesn't have packages of ramen noodles? Here's a fun way to use those noodles and surprise your friends.

PREP TIME:
18 MINUTES

COOLING TIME:
30 MINUTES

COOK TIME:
7 TO 8 MINUTES

Tip

The cooked buns can be wrapped individually in plastic wrap and stored in the refrigerator for up to 2 days. Alternatively, you can prepare them through step 3 and refrigerate overnight, then cook the buns immediately before assembling the sandwich.

* Two $3/4$-cup (175 mL) ramekins

1	package (3 oz/85 g) chicken- or beef-flavored ramen noodle soup	1
1	large egg	1
	Nonstick cooking spray	
	Olive oil	

1. Prepare ramen noodles according to package directions. Drain noodles and let cool to room temperature, about 15 minutes.

2. In a medium bowl, gently whisk egg. Stir in noodles until evenly coated.

3. Spray ramekins with cooking spray. Divide noodle mixture evenly between ramekins, pressing the noodles down into the ramekins. Cover the noodles with plastic wrap and place a heavy can or jar on top of the plastic wrap to weigh down the noodles. Refrigerate for 30 minutes.

4. Lightly coat a skillet with olive oil and heat over medium-high heat. Remove plastic wrap and invert ramekins to slide noodle buns onto skillet. Cook noodle buns for 4 to 5 minutes or until golden brown on the bottom. Turn the buns over and cook for 3 minutes or until firm, golden brown and hot in the center.

Variation

Stir 2 tsp (10 mL) chopped fresh chives in with the egg before adding the ramen noodles.

Meatloaf and Horseradish on Rye

A bit of horseradish adds some kick to leftover meatloaf in this hearty sandwich.

PREP TIME:

3 MINUTES

COOK TIME:

4 TO 5 MINUTES

Tip

Prepared horseradish can vary substantially in texture and taste. Refrigerated brands typically use only grated horseradish, vinegar and salt. They will be truer to taste and not as smooth as shelf-stable varieties, and can last for months in the refrigerator. Refrigerated horseradish also generally has fewer additives and unnatural ingredients.

◆ Preheat breakfast sandwich maker

2 tsp	prepared horseradish	10 mL
2	slices rye bread, cut into 4-inch (10 cm) rounds	2
1	½-inch (1 cm) thick slice meatloaf, cut to fit sandwich ring	1
	Nonstick cooking spray	
1	large egg	1

1. Spread horseradish on one side of each bread slice. Place one slice, spread side up, in bottom ring of sandwich maker. Top with meatloaf.

2. Lower the cooking plate and top ring. Lightly spray the plate with cooking spray, then crack the egg into the ring. Pierce top of egg yolk with a toothpick or plastic fork. Place the other bread slice, spread side down, on top of the egg.

3. Gently close the cover and cook for 4 to 5 minutes or until egg is cooked to your liking. Rotate cooking plate away from sandwich maker and lift rings. Use a plastic or nylon spatula to remove the sandwich. Serve immediately.

Italian Meatball Sandwich

Warm Italian meatballs bathed in tomato sauce and cheese make a filling sandwich that will be enjoyed by kids and adults alike.

Tips

Frozen cooked Italian-style meatballs are easy to use in this recipe. Heat them in the microwave for 1 minute, or according to the directions on the package, before slicing them and adding to your sandwich.

You may want to scrape out a little of the soft bread from the middle of the bottom half of the roll, creating a trench to hold your meatballs and sauce.

◆ Preheat breakfast sandwich maker

1	4-inch (10 cm) crusty bread roll, split in half	1
2	small cooked Italian-style meatballs (cherry tomato size), sliced	2
2 tbsp	marina or spaghetti sauce	30 mL
	Nonstick cooking spray	
1	large egg white	1
1½ tbsp	shredded Italian 3-cheese blend (Parmesan, Romano and Asiago)	22 mL

1. Place bottom half of roll, split side up, in bottom ring of sandwich maker. Top with meatballs and marinara sauce.

2. Lower the cooking plate and top ring. Lightly spray the plate with cooking spray, then add the egg white. Sprinkle with cheese blend. Place the other roll half, split side down, on top.

3. Gently close the cover and cook for 3 to 4 minutes or until egg white is cooked through and no longer translucent. Rotate cooking plate away from sandwich maker and lift rings. Use a plastic or nylon spatula to remove the sandwich. Serve immediately.

Sausage and Maple Bread Pudding Sandwich

This trendy breakfast sandwich uses slices of bread pudding, for the ultimate in decadence.

PREP TIME:

2 MINUTES

COOK TIME:

4 TO 5 MINUTES

Tips

You can drop the bread pudding directly from the ramekin into the sandwich maker. Tap the ramekin to loosen the pudding, then turn it upside down and release the bread pudding.

This sandwich is best eaten with a fork, as the bread pudding is soft and may crumble a bit.

◆ Preheat breakfast sandwich maker

2	slices Maple Bread Pudding (see recipe, opposite)	2
1	slice pepper Jack cheese	1
1	frozen cooked pork sausage patty	1
	Nonstick cooking spray	
1	large egg	1

1. Place one bread pudding slice in bottom ring of sandwich maker. Top with cheese and sausage.

2. Lower the cooking plate and top ring. Lightly spray the plate with cooking spray, then crack the egg into the ring. Pierce top of egg yolk with a toothpick or plastic fork. Place the remaining bread pudding slice on top of the egg.

3. Gently close the cover and cook for 4 to 5 minutes or until egg is cooked to your liking. Rotate cooking plate away from sandwich maker and lift rings. Use a plastic or nylon spatula to remove the sandwich. Serve immediately.

Maple Bread Pudding

This moist, sweet bread pudding is incredibly fast and easy, and makes a unique bread choice for divine breakfast sandwiches.

PREP TIME:
5 MINUTES

COOK TIME:
2 MINUTES

COOLING TIME:
5 MINUTES

Tips

Bread pudding is a great way to use up stale bread. Get creative by using a different variety of bread each time you make it. But make sure to choose a dense bread, as the pudding may get mushy with a softer one.

This bread pudding is also delicious all by itself, as a dessert. Try drizzling warm maple syrup or caramel sauce over top. Add a dollop of whipped cream for an even tastier treat.

* Two ¾-cup (175 mL) ramekins

	Nonstick cooking spray	
2	slices stale dense bread	2
1	large egg	1
2 tbsp	pure maple syrup	30 mL
2 tbsp	plain yogurt	30 mL
1 tbsp	butter, melted	15 mL
Pinch	ground cinnamon	Pinch

1. Lightly spray ramekins with cooking spray. Tear bread into small chunks and divide evenly between ramekins.

2. In a small bowl, whisk together eggs, maple syrup, yogurt, butter and cinnamon. Pour over bread chunks, moving the bread bits to make sure the egg mixture fills in openings around them. Do not stir.

3. Microwave on High for 2 minutes or until firm. Let cool for 5 minutes to absorb flavors and firm up.

Variation

Add 1 cooked sausage link, cut into 1-inch (2.5 cm) chunks, with the bread chunks in step 1. The result will be a stand-alone breakfast in a cup.

Pancetta and Provolone on Sourdough

Delicate pancetta, provolone, green onions and basil give this breakfast sandwich a refreshingly light taste.

PREP TIME:	
3 MINUTES	

COOK TIME:	
4 TO 5 MINUTES	

Tips

Cook pancetta as you would cook bacon. A small skillet makes it easier to get just the right doneness. To make sandwich preparation faster, cook a larger amount of pancetta in advance. Cooked pancetta can be stored in the refrigerator for up to 3 weeks.

If you are purchasing pancetta from the deli, ask them to cut it into 1-inch (2.5 cm) thick slices. This will make it easier to chop into nice size cubes for cooking.

♦ Preheat breakfast sandwich maker

2	slices sourdough bread, cut into 4-inch (10 cm) rounds	2
1	slice provolone cheese	1
2 tbsp	chopped cooked pancetta (see tips, at left)	30 mL
1 tsp	thinly sliced green onion	5 mL
	Nonstick cooking spray	
1	large egg	1
Pinch	chopped fresh basil (optional)	Pinch

1. Place one bread slice in bottom ring of sandwich maker. Top with cheese, pancetta and green onion.

2. Lower the cooking plate and top ring. Lightly spray the plate with cooking spray, then crack the egg into the ring. Pierce top of egg yolk with a toothpick or plastic fork. Sprinkle with basil (if using). Place the other bread slice on top of the egg.

3. Gently close the cover and cook for 4 to 5 minutes or until egg is cooked to your liking. Rotate cooking plate away from sandwich maker and lift rings. Use a plastic or nylon spatula to remove the sandwich. Serve immediately.

Variation

For a deeper, ham-like taste, substitute 2 to 3 thin slices of prosciutto for the pancetta.

Prosciutto and Asparagus Eggs Benedict

Nothing says gourmet breakfast like delicious eggs Benedict topped with asparagus spears.

PREP TIME:

2 MINUTES

COOK TIME:

4 TO 5 MINUTES

Tips

If you like your eggs to the soft poached stage, cook the sandwich for 3 to 4 minutes or just until the yolk is cooked soft and the white is no longer translucent.

You can wait to add the hollandaise sauce until after you remove the sandwich from the sandwich maker. If you do, warm the hollandaise in the microwave on High for 15 to 20 seconds before drizzling it over the egg. (Do not let the hollandaise start to bubble when heating.)

◆ Preheat breakfast sandwich maker

½	English muffin	½
2	thin slices prosciutto	2
5	frozen cut asparagus spears	5
	Nonstick cooking spray	
1	large egg	1
2 tbsp	hollandaise sauce	30 mL

1. Place English muffin half, split side up, in bottom ring of sandwich maker. Top with prosciutto and asparagus.

2. Lower the cooking plate and top ring. Lightly spray the plate with cooking spray, then crack the egg into the ring. Pierce top of egg yolk with a toothpick or plastic fork. Drizzle hollandaise sauce over the egg.

3. Gently close the cover and cook for 4 to 5 minutes or until egg is cooked to your liking. Rotate cooking plate away from sandwich maker and lift rings. Use a plastic or nylon spatula to remove the sandwich. Serve immediately.

Antipasto Breakfast Sandwich

Antipasto means "before the meal," but in my take on this Italian appetizer, it means "before the day." A wide variety of marinated vegetables, cured meats and cheeses can be used in antipasto. Explore different options and get creative with combinations — this sandwich never gets boring.

PREP TIME:
6 MINUTES

COOK TIME:
4 TO 5 MINUTES

Tips

I like this sandwich open-face, but you can add another slice of sourdough on top of the egg mixture if you prefer.

Mix up the vegetable combinations you use in this sandwich. You can often find pickled or marinated mixed vegetables in a jar at the grocery store, making sandwich prep even easier.

♦ Preheat breakfast sandwich maker

1	large egg	1
2 tsp	chopped tomatoes	10 mL
1	slice sourdough bread, cut into 4-inch (10 cm) rounds	1
2	ciliegine (fresh mozzarella) balls, sliced	2
2	thin slices prosciutto	2
1 tbsp	diced drained oil-packed or marinated artichoke hearts	15 mL
	Nonstick cooking spray	
2 tsp	sliced black olives	10 mL

1. In a small bowl, gently whisk egg. Stir in tomatoes. Set aside.

2. Place bread slice in bottom ring of sandwich maker. Top with cheese, prosciutto and artichokes.

3. Lower the cooking plate and top ring. Lightly spray the plate with cooking spray, then pour in the egg mixture. Sprinkle with olives.

4. Gently close the cover and cook for 4 to 5 minutes or until egg is cooked to your liking. Rotate cooking plate away from sandwich maker and lift rings. Use a plastic or nylon spatula to remove the sandwich. Serve immediately.

Monte Cristo Sandwich

While I love Monte Cristo sandwiches, about the only way I can get one that isn't soggy or greasy is to order it in a trusted restaurant. But now I can enjoy a perfect sandwich at home in just minutes!

PREP TIME:
2 MINUTES

COOK TIME:
4 TO 5 MINUTES

Tip

For crispier French toast, toast the slices before adding them to the sandwich maker.

Variations

Use sliced turkey in place of the ham. It's a leaner alternative and a great way to use up leftovers.

Use both ham and turkey, but keep the combined quantity to 3 oz (90 g).

♦ Preheat breakfast sandwich maker

2	slices frozen French toast, cut into 4-inch (10 cm) rounds	2
1	slice Swiss cheese	1
2 oz	sliced deli ham (2 to 3 thin slices)	60 g
	Nonstick cooking spray	
1	large egg	1
	Confectioners' (icing) sugar (optional)	
	Strawberry, raspberry or grape jelly (optional)	

1. Place a slice of French toast in bottom ring of sandwich maker. Top with cheese and ham.

2. Lower the cooking plate and top ring. Lightly spray the plate with cooking spray, then crack the egg into the ring. Pierce top of egg yolk with a toothpick or plastic fork. Place the other French toast slice on top of the egg.

3. Gently close the cover and cook for 4 to 5 minutes or until egg is cooked to your liking. Rotate cooking plate away from sandwich maker and lift rings. Use a plastic or nylon spatula to remove the sandwich. Serve immediately, lightly sprinkled with confectioners' sugar, if desired, and with strawberry jelly on the side for dipping, if desired.

Ham, Stilton and Pear on Brioche

Stilton is a blue cheese that is only produced in three counties in England. A little goes a long way, but it is so versatile, you are sure to find many uses for this prized cheese.

PREP TIME:
3 MINUTES

COOK TIME:
4 TO 5 MINUTES

Tips

Stilton freezes beautifully, unlike many cheeses, and you can grate or crumble it from frozen. It makes for a great last-minute addition to sandwiches or salads.

A sweet dessert wine or port would go very nicely with this sandwich.

◆ Preheat breakfast sandwich maker

1	4-inch (10 cm) brioche bun, split in half	1
1	slice cooked ham (about ¼ inch/0.5 cm thick)	1
¼	thinly sliced pear	¼
2 tsp	crumbled Stilton cheese	10 mL
	Nonstick cooking spray	
1	large egg	1

1. Place bottom half of bun, split side up, in bottom ring of sandwich maker. Top with ham, pear and cheese.

2. Lower the cooking plate and top ring. Lightly spray the plate with cooking spray, then crack the egg into the ring. Pierce top of egg yolk with a toothpick or plastic fork. Place the other bun half on top of the egg.

3. Gently close the cover and cook for 4 to 5 minutes or until egg is cooked to your liking. Rotate cooking plate away from sandwich maker and lift rings. Use a plastic or nylon spatula to remove the sandwich. Serve immediately.

Muffuletta Sandwich

Here, a variety of meats, cheese and olives are packed into a hearty New Orleans–style picnic sandwich.

PREP TIME:
5 MINUTES

COOK TIME:
4 TO 5 MINUTES

Tips

The cooking plate will be very hot when it is rotated away from the machine. Use caution when lowering the top ring and adding the roll half, and be careful not to touch the plate at any time during the cooking process.

You can fully assemble the sandwich, wrap it tightly in plastic wrap and refrigerate it for up to 24 hours. Many muffuletta aficionados like to do this so the sandwich flavors have a chance to combine.

◆ Preheat breakfast sandwich maker

1	4-inch (10 cm) muffuletta roll or Italian roll, split in half	1
2 tsp	chopped pitted green olives	10 mL
2 tsp	chopped kalamata olives	10 mL
1 tbsp	chopped drained oil-packed roasted red bell peppers	15 mL
1	slice deli ham	1
1	slice Genoa salami	1
1	slice mortadella	1
1	slice provolone cheese	1
1	slice mozzarella cheese	1

1. Carefully hollow out a small area in the center of the bottom roll half. Place green olives, kalamata olives and roasted peppers in the hollow area. Place roll half, hollow side up, in bottom ring of sandwich maker. Top with ham, salami, mortadella, provolone and mozzarella.

2. Rotate cooking plate away from top ring of sandwich maker (see tip, at left). Carefully lower top ring, with cooking plate extended away from the sandwich maker. Gently place the other roll half on top of the sandwich.

3. Gently close the cover (do not push it down) and cook for 4 to 5 minutes or until sandwich is warmed through and cheese is melted. Lift rings and use a plastic or nylon spatula to remove the sandwich. Serve immediately.

Grilled Chicken with Monterey Jack and Chipotle Mayo

Lean grilled chicken breast pairs with spicy chipotle mayo to create a flavorful sandwich for lunch or dinner.

PREP TIME:

2 MINUTES

COOK TIME:

4 TO 5 MINUTES

Tips

Use leftover grilled chicken breast strips if you have them on hand, or purchase refrigerated or frozen grilled chicken breast strips. An easy way to pick up just the right amount is to get them at the salad counter at the grocery store.

For a lighter sandwich, omit the egg. Place the top half of the roll directly on the cooking plate to toast it.

Chipotle mayonnaise has become such a popular addition to sandwiches, tacos and burgers that you can find it ready-made in your grocery store.

◆ Preheat breakfast sandwich maker

1 tbsp	chipotle mayonnaise (see tip, at left)	15 mL
1	4-inch (10 cm) Kaiser roll, split in half	1
1	slice Monterey Jack cheese	1
2 to 3	grilled chicken breast strips	2 to 3
	Nonstick cooking spray	
1	large egg	1

1. Spread mayonnaise on bottom half of roll. Place roll half, spread side up, in bottom ring of sandwich maker. Top with cheese and chicken.

2. Lower the cooking plate and top ring. Lightly spray the plate with cooking spray, then crack the egg into the ring. Pierce top of egg yolk with a toothpick or plastic fork. Place the other roll half on top of the egg.

3. Gently close the cover and cook for 4 to 5 minutes or until egg is cooked to your liking. Rotate cooking plate away from sandwich maker and lift rings. Use a plastic or nylon spatula to remove the sandwich. Serve immediately.

Leftover Turkey and Cranberry Relish Sandwich

This down-home combination of autumn comfort foods is the perfect way to use up your leftover turkey feast fixings.

PREP TIME:

2 MINUTES

COOK TIME:

4 TO 5 MINUTES

Tips

Either dark or white meat works well in this recipe. Just pick your favorite. If you are using leftover turkey leg meat, be careful to remove the white tendons along with the bone.

If you serve jellied cranberry sauce instead of cranberry relish with your turkey dinner, that will also work nicely with this sandwich. I would use one thin slice of the jelly.

• Preheat breakfast sandwich maker

2 tsp	butter, softened	10 mL
1	4-inch (10 cm) dinner roll, split in half	1
2 tsp	cranberry relish	10 mL
1	slice Monterey Jack cheese	1
2 to 3	slices leftover roasted turkey	2 to 3
	Nonstick cooking spray	
1	large egg	1

1. Spread butter over split sides of roll. Place bottom roll half, spread side up, in bottom ring of sandwich maker. Top with cranberry relish, cheese and turkey.

2. Lower the cooking plate and top ring. Lightly spray the plate with cooking spray, then crack the egg into the ring. Pierce top of egg yolk with a toothpick or plastic fork. Place the other roll half, spread side down, on top of the egg.

3. Gently close the cover and cook for 4 to 5 minutes or until egg is cooked to your liking. Rotate cooking plate away from sandwich maker and lift rings. Use a plastic or nylon spatula to remove the sandwich. Serve immediately.

Mediterranean Tuna Sandwich

This combination of ingredients reminds me of the wonderful appetizer bruschetta, but proponents of the Mediterranean diet will enjoy this sandwich anytime.

PREP TIME:

5 MINUTES

COOK TIME:

3 TO 4 MINUTES

Tip

If you omit the bread and egg white, this same heart-healthy combination of ingredients works equally well on top of mixed greens for a refreshing salad.

- Preheat breakfast sandwich maker

2	slices French bread, cut into 4-inch (10 cm) rounds if necessary	2
	Olive oil	
½	can (5 oz/142 g) water-packed albacore tuna, drained	½
1 tbsp	sliced black olives	15 mL
2 tbsp	chopped tomato	30 mL
	Nonstick cooking spray	
1	large egg white	1
	Crumbled feta cheese	

1. Place one bread slice in bottom ring of sandwich maker. Drizzle lightly with olive oil. Top with tuna, olives and tomato.

2. Lower the cooking plate and top ring. Lightly spray the plate with cooking spray, then add the egg white. Sprinkle with cheese. Place the other bread slice on top.

3. Gently close the cover and cook for 3 to 4 minutes or until egg white is cooked through and no longer translucent. Rotate cooking plate away from sandwich maker and lift rings. Use a plastic or nylon spatula to remove the sandwich. Serve immediately.

Variation

For a milder flavor, substitute sliced fresh mozzarella — either the cherry-size balls known as ciliegine or the slightly larger balls called bocconcini — for the crumbled feta.

Shrimp Creole on a Biscuit

Don't be deterred by the longer list of ingredients here, because this sandwich is easy to make for two.

PREP TIME:
12 MINUTES

COOK TIME:
4 TO 5 MINUTES

Tip

I like to make this dish for two. Not only is it a great treat, but I am able to use the full can of shrimp and all I need to do is double the other ingredients. Preparation doesn't take any longer, but the cooking time for the sandwiches is, of course, double.

• Preheat breakfast sandwich maker

1 tbsp	butter	15 mL
1 tbsp	chopped celery	15 mL
1 tbsp	chopped onion	15 mL
1/4 tsp	minced garlic	1 mL
2 tsp	ketchup	10 mL
Dash	hot pepper sauce	Dash
1/2	can (4 oz/113 g) medium shrimp, drained	1/2
1	large egg	1
2 tsp	sliced green onion	10 mL
1	baking powder biscuit, split in half	1
	Nonstick cooking spray	

1. In a small skillet, melt butter over medium heat. Add celery, onion and garlic; cook, stirring, for about 5 minutes or until softened. Remove from heat and stir in ketchup and hot pepper sauce. Gently stir in shrimp. Set aside.

2. In a small bowl, gently whisk egg. Stir in green onions. Set aside.

3. Place bottom half of biscuit, split side up, in bottom ring of sandwich maker. Top with shrimp mixture.

4. Lower the cooking plate and top ring. Lightly spray the plate with cooking spray, then pour in the egg mixture. Place the other biscuit half, split side down, on top of the egg.

5. Gently close the cover and cook for 4 to 5 minutes or until egg is cooked to your liking. Rotate cooking plate away from sandwich maker and lift rings. Use a plastic or nylon spatula to remove the sandwich. Serve immediately.

International Flavors

◇◇◇

Spicy Peanut Pork and Pea Pods on Brioche

Inspiration for this recipe came from my local produce market, which always has a delicious sampling of fresh pea pods for dipping in a spicy peanut sauce. Spicy peanut sauce is used in a variety of ways in Asian cuisines and works particularly well in this sandwich.

PREP TIME:

3 MINUTES

COOK TIME:

4 TO 5 MINUTES

Tips

For best results, choose younger peas that have been harvested early in the season.

Sugar snap peas will also work in this recipe but may be a bit tougher.

The spicy peanut sauce can be used as a condiment in many sandwiches, as a dipping sauce for crisp vegetables or satays, or as a dressing for chopped mixed cabbage salads.

◆ Preheat breakfast sandwich maker

1 tbsp	spicy peanut sauce	15 mL
1	4-inch (10 cm) brioche bun, split in half	1
4	snow peas, trimmed	4
½	cooked small smoked boneless pork chop, sliced	½
	Nonstick cooking spray	
1	large egg	1

1. Spread peanut sauce on bottom half of bun. Place bun, spread side up, in bottom ring of sandwich maker. Top with snow peas and pork.

2. Lower the cooking plate and top ring. Lightly spray the plate with cooking spray, then crack the egg into the ring. Pierce top of egg yolk with a toothpick or plastic fork. Place the other bun half, split side down, on top of the egg.

3. Gently close the cover and cook for 4 to 5 minutes or until egg is cooked to your liking. Rotate cooking plate away from sandwich maker and lift rings. Use a plastic or nylon spatula to remove the sandwich. Serve immediately.

Five-Spice Pork on a Baguette

Preparing this Chinese-inspired recipe takes very little time, but you do need to plan ahead so the marinade can work its magic, tenderizing and flavoring the meat.

MARINATING TIME:
2 HOURS

PREP TIME:
10 MINUTES

COOK TIME:
4 TO 5 MINUTES

Tip

Chinese five-spice, an aromatic blend of ground cinnamon, star anise, ginger, fennel and cloves, is readily available in supermarkets. It gives a slightly sweet and pungent flavor to dishes.

3 oz	pork cutlet or boneless pork loin roast, cut into strips	90 g
1½ tsp	Chinese five-spice powder	7 mL
1 tbsp	soy sauce	15 mL
2 tsp	olive oil	10 mL
1	4-inch (10 cm) long petit baguette, split in half	1
	Nonstick cooking spray	
1	large egg	1

1. Place pork in a sealable plastic bag. Add five-spice powder, soy sauce and oil. Seal bag and shake lightly to blend ingredients. Refrigerate for at least 2 hours, to blend the flavors and tenderize the meat.

2. Preheat breakfast sandwich maker.

3. Remove pork from marinade, discarding marinade. Heat a small pan over medium heat. Cook pork strips, stirring and turning frequently, for 4 to 6 minutes or until just a hint of pink remains inside.

4. Place bottom half of baguette, split side up, in bottom ring of sandwich maker. Top with pork.

5. Lower the cooking plate and top ring. Lightly spray the plate with cooking spray, then crack the egg into the ring. Pierce top of egg yolk with a toothpick or plastic fork. Place the other baguette half, split side down, on top of the egg.

6. Gently close the cover and cook for 4 to 5 minutes or until egg is cooked to your liking. Rotate cooking plate away from sandwich maker and lift rings. Use a plastic or nylon spatula to remove the sandwich. Serve immediately.

Tamale-Style Peppery Pork on Cornbread

Traditional Mexican tamales can be time-consuming to make. With this recipe, you can enjoy the texture and flavors of a Mexican tamale in less than 10 minutes.

PREP TIME:

3 MINUTES

COOK TIME:

4 TO 5 MINUTES

Tip

Cornbread can be very dense or can have a more crumbly texture. A denser, skillet type of cornbread works better in this recipe.

The cornbread makes this sandwich a little more delicate to handle. Be careful when removing it from the sandwich maker. It is best eaten with a fork, as you would a traditional tamale.

◆ Preheat breakfast sandwich maker

	Nonstick cooking spray	
2	thin slices cornbread, cut into 4 inch (10 cm) rounds	2
1	slice pepper Jack cheese	1
2 tbsp	shredded cooked pork	30 mL
1	large egg	1
	Salsa	

1. Lightly spray bottom plate of sandwich maker with cooking spray. Place one cornbread slice in bottom ring. Top with cheese and pork.

2. Lower the cooking plate and top ring. Lightly spray the plate with cooking spray, then crack the egg into the ring. Pierce top of egg yolk with a toothpick or plastic fork. Place the other cornbread slice on top of the egg.

3. Gently close the cover and cook for 4 to 5 minutes or until egg is cooked to your liking. Rotate cooking plate away from sandwich maker and lift rings. Use a plastic or nylon spatula to remove the sandwich. Serve immediately, with salsa on the side.

The Cuban Sandwich

There is some debate about the origins of the Cuban sandwich, but everyone agrees that it must include roast pork, ham, Swiss cheese, mustard and pickles.

PREP TIME:
3 MINUTES

COOK TIME:
4 TO 5 MINUTES

Variations

You can omit the egg in this sandwich if you want a more traditional Cuban sandwich.

Add a slice of salami along with the pork and ham. In some areas of Florida, where this sandwich is famous, salami is added thanks to the influence of Italian immigrants who lived near the expat Cubans in the early settlements.

♦ Preheat breakfast sandwich maker

2 tbsp	prepared mustard	30 mL
2	slices French bread, cut into 4-inch (10 cm) rounds if necessary	2
1	thin slice deli or leftover roast pork	1
1	slice Swiss cheese	1
3	crosswise slices dill pickle	3
1	thin slice deli ham	1
	Nonstick cooking spray	
1	large egg	1

1. Spread mustard on one side of each bread slice. Place one slice, spread side up, in bottom ring of sandwich maker. Top with pork, cheese, pickles and ham.

2. Lower the cooking plate and top ring. Lightly spray the plate with cooking spray, then crack the egg into the ring. Pierce top of egg yolk with a toothpick or plastic fork. Place the other bread slice, spread side down, on top of the egg.

3. Gently close the cover and cook for 4 to 5 minutes or until egg is cooked to your liking. Rotate cooking plate away from sandwich maker and lift rings. Use a plastic or nylon spatula to remove the sandwich. Serve immediately.

Hawaiian Ham Sandwich

When you bite into this sandwich, packed with savory ham and sweet, juicy pineapple, you'll feel like you've been transported to a luau.

PREP TIME:

2 MINUTES

COOK TIME:

3 TO 4 MINUTES

Tips

A sweet Hawaiian roll is a wonderful option for this sandwich instead of the soft bread roll. It will add a nice sweetness, making the Hawaiian flavor experience complete.

Canned sliced pineapple makes this dish incredibly simple. You can use either sweetened or unsweetened pineapple. Or use fresh pineapple, if you happen to have it on hand.

◆ Preheat breakfast sandwich maker

2 tsp	butter	10 mL
1	4-inch (10 cm) soft bread roll, split in half	1
2 to 3	slices deli ham	2 to 3
1	slice pineapple	1
	Nonstick cooking spray	
1	large egg white	1

1. Spread butter on split sides of roll. Place bottom half of roll, split side up, in bottom ring of sandwich maker. Top with ham and pineapple.

2. Lower the cooking plate and top ring. Lightly spray the plate with cooking spray, then add the egg white. Place the other roll half, spread side down, on top of the egg white.

3. Gently close the cover and cook for 3 to 4 minutes or until egg white is cooked through and no longer translucent. Rotate cooking plate away from sandwich maker and lift rings. Use a plastic or nylon spatula to remove the sandwich. Serve immediately.

Variation

Sprinkle some shredded coconut on top of the pineapple, for a piña colada flare.

Provençal Avocado and Garlic Aïoli Sandwich

The creamy garlic aïoli flavoring this scrumptious bacon, avocado and Cheddar sandwich will have you feeling like you've been swept away to the Provençal region of France.

PREP TIME:
3 MINUTES

COOK TIME:
4 TO 5 MINUTES

Tips

Look for prepared garlic aïoli in the condiment section of your grocery store. If you can't find it, make your own by whisking together 1 clove minced garlic, a pinch of kosher salt, $\frac{1}{4}$ cup (60 mL) mayonnaise, 1 tbsp (15 mL) olive oil and $1\frac{1}{2}$ tsp (7 mL) lemon juice, to make about $\frac{1}{3}$ cup (75 mL) aïoli. Store in an airtight container in the refrigerator for up to 1 week.

A basil pesto aïoli or lemon herb aïoli will also provide Provençal flavors.

• Preheat breakfast sandwich maker

1 tbsp	garlic aïoli	15 mL
2	slices multigrain bread, cut into 4-inch (10 cm) rounds	2
1	slice Cheddar cheese	1
2	slices thick-cut bacon, cooked crisp	2
$\frac{1}{4}$	small avocado, sliced	$\frac{1}{4}$
	Nonstick cooking spray	
1	large egg	1
1	slice red onion, separated into rings	1

1. Spread aïoli on one side of one bread slice. Place bread slice, spread side up, in bottom ring of sandwich maker. Top with cheese. Break bacon into pieces that fit in the ring and add on top of the cheese. Top with avocado.

2. Lower the cooking plate and top ring. Lightly spray the plate with cooking spray, then crack the egg into the ring. Pierce top of egg yolk with a toothpick or plastic fork. Top with onion rings. Place the other bread slice on top of the onion rings.

3. Gently close the cover and cook for 4 to 5 minutes or until egg is cooked to your liking. Rotate cooking plate away from sandwich maker and lift rings. Use a plastic or nylon spatula to remove the sandwich. Serve immediately.

Kickin' Hot Bacon and Cucumber Sandwich

Harissa, a chile-based paste used in North African cuisine, provides the kick in this sandwich.

PREP TIME:

3 MINUTES

COOK TIME:

4 TO 5 MINUTES

Tip

Harissa paste is a fiery hot seasoning made with a variety of dried chile peppers, garlic, coriander, caraway and cumin. It comes in cans, jars and tubes. Check the type of peppers used in your mix, as they can change the heat and smokiness level of the paste substantially.

• Preheat breakfast sandwich maker

2 tsp	harissa paste	10 mL
2	slices flatbread, cut into 4-inch (10 cm) rounds	2
3	slices thick-cut bacon, cooked crisp	3
2 to 3	slices cucumber	2 to 3
	Nonstick cooking spray	
1	large egg	1

1. Spread harissa on one side of one or both flatbread slices. Place one slice, spread side up, in bottom ring of sandwich maker. Break bacon into pieces that fit in the ring and add on top of the flatbread. Top with cucumber.

2. Lower the cooking plate and top ring. Lightly spray the plate with cooking spray, then crack the egg into the ring. Pierce top of egg yolk with a toothpick or plastic fork. Place the other flatbread slice, spread side up, on top of the egg.

3. Gently close the cover and cook for 4 to 5 minutes or until egg is cooked to your liking. Rotate cooking plate away from sandwich maker and lift rings. Use a plastic or nylon spatula to remove the sandwich. Serve immediately.

Variations

Substitute 2 to 3 slices of cooked lamb or pork, or 2 oz (60 g) cooked fish, for the bacon.

To tame the heat slightly, mix the harissa paste with a dollop of plain yogurt before spreading it on the bread.

Chorizo Egg Torta

Creamy gooey goodness from the avocado and cheeses adds wonderful highlights to the smoky Spanish chorizo.

PREP TIME:

4 MINUTES

COOK TIME:

4 TO 5 MINUTES

Tips

Have the deli slice the chorizo for you, or buy a whole cured sausage for slicing. Chorizo slices make wonderful tapas.

If you purchase fresh Spanish chorizo, you will need to cook it before using it here.

♦ Preheat breakfast sandwich maker

2	slices flatbread, cut into 4-inch (10 cm) rounds	2
2 to 3	thin slices cured Spanish chorizo sausage	2 to 3
½	avocado, sliced	½
2 tbsp	shredded Monterey Jack cheese	30 mL
	Nonstick cooking spray	
1	large egg, whisked	1
1 tbsp	crumbled feta cheese	15 mL

1. Place one flatbread slice in bottom ring of sandwich maker. Top with chorizo, avocado and Monterey Jack.

2. Lower the cooking plate and top ring. Lightly spray the plate with cooking spray, then pour in the egg. Sprinkle with feta. Place the other flatbread slice on top.

3. Gently close the cover and cook for 4 to 5 minutes or until egg is cooked to your liking. Rotate cooking plate away from sandwich maker and lift rings. Use a plastic or nylon spatula to remove the sandwich. Serve immediately.

Variation

If you don't have flatbread on hand, substitute an English muffin, split in half.

Replace the feta cheese with queso fresco, for a lighter taste and a hint of sweetness.

Garam Masala Chicken on Pita

An aromatic blend of garam masala, chicken and cool cucumbers give this pita sandwich an air of Indian mystique.

PREP TIME:
5 MINUTES

COOK TIME:
4 TO 5 MINUTES

Tips

Garam masala is often said to be spicy, but that's because of the intensity of flavors and the complex variety of spices used, not the heat. The mixture of spices in garam masala varies across India depending upon regional tastes and home recipes. You can find garam masala blends in the spice section of most supermarkets.

When I use frozen cooked chicken strips for this recipe, I thaw them first so the flavors of the garam masala blend better.

◆ Preheat breakfast sandwich maker

2 to 3	cooked chicken strips, chopped	2 to 3
2 tbsp	chopped cucumber	30 mL
1 tsp	garam masala	5 mL
Dash	olive oil	Dash
2 tsp	plain yogurt	10 mL
1	small pita, cut into a 4-inch (10 cm) round	1
	Nonstick cooking spray	
1	large egg	1
2 tsp	sliced green onion (optional)	10 mL

1. In a small bowl, gently toss together chicken, cucumber, garam masala and oil.

2. Spread yogurt on one side of pita. Place pita, spread side up, in bottom ring of sandwich maker. Top with chicken mixture.

3. Lower the cooking plate and top ring. Lightly spray the plate with cooking spray, then crack the egg into the ring. Pierce top of egg yolk with a toothpick or plastic fork. Sprinkle with green onion (if using).

4. Gently close the cover and cook for 4 to 5 minutes or until egg is cooked to your liking. Rotate cooking plate away from sandwich maker and lift rings. Use a plastic or nylon spatula to remove the sandwich. Serve immediately.

Indian Mango Chicken Sandwich

The spicy and sweet combination of flavors in this sandwich makes for a delicious midday snack or a light lunch.

PREP TIME:
5 MINUTES

COOK TIME:
4 TO 5 MINUTES

Tip

If you have leftover cooked chicken, use ¼ cup (60 mL) chopped chicken instead of the deli slices.

◆ Preheat breakfast sandwich maker

¼ cup	diced mango	60 mL
¼ tsp	hot pepper flakes	1 mL
2	slices sourdough bread, cut into 4-inch (10 cm) rounds	2
2 to 3	slices deli chicken breast	2 to 3
2 to 3	thin slices cucumber	2 to 3
	Nonstick cooking spray	
1	large egg	1
1 tbsp	sliced green onion	15 mL

1. In a small bowl, combine mango and hot pepper flakes until mango is evenly coated.

2. Place one bread slice in bottom ring of sandwich maker. Top with mango mixture, chicken and cucumber.

3. Lower the cooking plate and top ring. Lightly spray the plate with cooking spray, then crack the egg into the ring. Pierce top of egg yolk with a toothpick or plastic fork. Sprinkle with green onion. Place the other bread slice on top.

4. Gently close the cover and cook for 4 to 5 minutes or until egg is cooked to your liking. Rotate cooking plate away from sandwich maker and lift rings. Use a plastic or nylon spatula to remove the sandwich. Serve immediately.

Variation

Substitute mango chutney for the mango and hot pepper flakes, for an even more robust taste.

Sweet and Hot Chicken on Flatbread

Contrasting yet complementary flavors abound in this South Asia–inspired sandwich.

Tips

You can use a little curry paste instead of powder, if you prefer. Spread it on the flatbread along with the yogurt. Curry paste has a much stronger flavor than powder, so use it sparingly.

Greek yogurt works best here. If you only have regular yogurt, you can make your own Greek yogurt. Place a sieve lined with cheesecloth over a glass container. Cover with plastic wrap and let stand in the refrigerator for about 8 hours to let the liquid (whey) drain off.

• Preheat breakfast sandwich maker

1	large egg	1
1 tsp	curry powder	5 mL
2 tbsp	plain Greek yogurt	30 mL
2	slices flatbread, cut into 4-inch (10 cm) rounds	2
2 to 3	slices deli chicken breast	2 to 3
¼	green apple, sliced	¼
1 tbsp	raisins	15 mL
	Nonstick cooking spray	
1 tsp	dried cilantro	5 mL

1. In a small bowl, gently whisk together egg and curry powder. Set aside.

2. Spread yogurt on one side of both flatbread slices. Place one slice, spread side up, in bottom ring of sandwich maker. Top with chicken and apple. Sprinkle with raisins.

3. Lower the cooking plate and top ring. Lightly spray the plate with cooking spray, then pour in the egg mixture. Sprinkle with cilantro. Place the other flatbread slice, spread side down, on top of the egg.

4. Gently close the cover and cook for 4 to 5 minutes or until egg is cooked to your liking. Rotate cooking plate away from sandwich maker and lift rings. Use a plastic or nylon spatula to remove the sandwich. Serve immediately.

Mediterranean Turkey Sandwich

This rich blend of Mediterranean flavors will have you dreaming of floating in the Aegean Sea.

PREP TIME:
4 MINUTES

COOK TIME:
4 TO 5 MINUTES

Tips

You can purchase sun-dried tomatoes dry or packed in oil. Either will be fine for this recipe. If I use tomatoes packed in oil, I like to brush a little of the oil on the flatbread. If you use dried, you could also just brush a little olive oil on the flatbread.

This sandwich is a great way to use up any leftover turkey you may have on hand.

♦ Preheat breakfast sandwich maker

2	slices flatbread, cut into 4-inch (10 cm) rounds	2
2 tbsp	crumbled feta cheese	30 mL
2 to 3	slices deli turkey	2 to 3
1	sun-dried tomato, sliced	1
1 tbsp	sliced black olives	15 mL
	Nonstick cooking spray	
1	large egg	1

1. Place one flatbread slice in bottom ring of sandwich maker. Top with feta, turkey, sun-dried tomato and olives.

2. Lower the cooking plate and top ring. Lightly spray the plate with cooking spray, then crack the egg into the ring. Pierce top of egg yolk with a toothpick or plastic fork. Place the other flatbread slice on top of the egg.

3. Gently close the cover and cook for 4 to 5 minutes or until egg is cooked to your liking. Rotate cooking plate away from sandwich maker and lift rings. Use a plastic or nylon spatula to remove the sandwich. Serve immediately.

Tuna and Olives on French Bread

This sandwich originated along the southern Mediterranean coast of France, where it is known as *pan bagnat*, meaning "bathed bread." This is my take on the more traditional recipe. It makes a wonderful summertime sandwich.

PREP TIME:
5 MINUTES

COOK TIME:
4 TO 5 MINUTES

Tips

If you want to use something other than a French bread roll, make sure you use a roll with a hard crust. This will help the olive oil and juices stay in the sandwich.

The traditional Provençal sandwich calls for scooping out a little of the softer bread in the middle of the roll to hold in more of the liquid and ingredients. Give this a try with the bottom half of the roll.

◆ Preheat breakfast sandwich maker

1	can (3 oz/85 g) water-packed tuna, drained	1
1½ tbsp	sliced black olives	22 mL
2 tbsp	diced tomato	30 mL
2 tbsp	olive oil, divided	30 mL
Pinch	salt	Pinch
Pinch	freshly ground black pepper	Pinch
1	French bread roll, split in half	1
	Nonstick cooking spray	
1	large egg	1
1	slice mozzarella cheese	1

1. In a small bowl, combine tuna, olives, tomato, 1 tbsp (15 mL) oil, salt and pepper.

2. Brush the remaining olive oil over split sides of roll. Place bottom half of roll, oil side up, in bottom ring of sandwich maker. Top with tuna mixture.

3. Lower the cooking plate and top ring. Lightly spray the plate with cooking spray, then crack the egg into the ring. Pierce top of egg yolk with a toothpick or plastic fork. Top with cheese. Place the other roll half, oil side down, on top of the cheese.

4. Gently close the cover and cook for 4 to 5 minutes or until egg is cooked to your liking. Rotate cooking plate away from sandwich maker and lift rings. Use a plastic or nylon spatula to remove the sandwich. Serve immediately.

Spicy Thai Chile Tuna Medley

If you love Thai food, this sandwich will give you a quick fix to start your day or will make a nice accompaniment to hot-and-sour soup for dinner.

Tips

The Thai spice blend I buy from my local store contains sesame seeds, paprika, coriander, garlic, onion, cilantro, basil, red pepper, cinnamon, nutmeg, natural shrimp flavor and lemon oil. Given all those ingredients, I much prefer to buy a spice blend than make my own.

You can use Thai curry paste instead of the Thai spice blend. If you choose one of the hotter curry pastes, omit the hot pepper flakes.

◆ Preheat breakfast sandwich maker

1	can (3 oz/85 g) water-packed tuna, drained	1
1 tsp	hot pepper flakes	5 mL
2 tsp	Thai spice blend	10 mL
1	English muffin, split in half	1
	Nonstick cooking spray	
1	large egg	1

1. In a small bowl, combine tuna, hot pepper flakes and Thai spice blend.

2. Place one English muffin half, split side up, in bottom ring of sandwich maker. Top with tuna mixture.

3. Lower the cooking plate and top ring. Lightly spray the plate with cooking spray, then crack the egg into the ring. Pierce top of egg yolk with a toothpick or plastic fork. Place the other muffin half, split side down, on top of the egg.

4. Gently close the cover and cook for 4 to 5 minutes or until egg is cooked to your liking. Rotate cooking plate away from sandwich maker and lift rings. Use a plastic or nylon spatula to remove the sandwich. Serve immediately.

Cajun Shrimp Sandwich

Cajun shrimp is typically served on a bed of rice, but works just as well on a crusty roll with a fried egg.

Tips

If you have time, chill the Cajun mayonnaise in the refrigerator for 20 minutes (or longer). The flavors become better over time.

Since shrimp is high in cholesterol, you can omit the egg or use 2 egg whites if you are looking to reduce your cholesterol intake.

♦ Preheat breakfast sandwich maker

2 tbsp	mayonnaise	30 mL
1 tsp	Cajun seasoning	5 mL
1 tsp	paprika	5 mL
Dash	hot pepper sauce	Dash
1	4-inch (10 cm) crusty bread roll, split in half	1
1	can (4 oz/113 g) small or medium shrimp, drained	1
1	slice tomato	1
	Nonstick cooking spray	
1	large egg	1

1. In a small bowl, combine mayonnaise, Cajun seasoning, paprika and hot pepper sauce until well blended.

2. Spread mayonnaise mixture on split sides of roll. Place bottom half of roll, spread side up, in sandwich maker. Top with shrimp and tomato.

3. Lower the cooking plate and top ring. Lightly spray the plate with cooking spray, then crack the egg into the ring. Pierce top of egg yolk with a toothpick or plastic fork. Place the other roll half, spread side down, on top of the egg.

4. Gently close the cover and cook for 4 to 5 minutes or until egg is cooked to your liking. Rotate cooking plate away from sandwich maker and lift rings. Use a plastic or nylon spatula to remove the sandwich. Serve immediately.

Chicken Fajita

Here it is: the easiest fajita you will ever make. Enjoy this Tex-Mex treat with chips and salsa and a cold drink while watching your favorite televised sporting event.

PREP TIME:
5 MINUTES

COOK TIME:
4 TO 5 MINUTES

Tip

My favorite trick for making this fajita is to purchase all of the ingredients from the salad bar at my local grocery store. I can find cooked chicken strips, all the diced ingredients and even the shredded cheese ready-made. It is so fast and easy!

Variations

Substitute cooked beef or pork strips for the chicken.

Add sliced black olives or diced tomatoes on top of the meat and cheese.

♦ Preheat breakfast sandwich maker

1 tbsp	chopped onion	15 mL
1 tbsp	chopped green bell pepper	15 mL
1 tbsp	chopped red bell pepper	15 mL
Pinch	ground cumin	Pinch
Pinch	salt	Pinch
2	4-inch (10 cm) flour tortillas	2
2 to 3	cooked chicken strips	2 to 3
2 tbsp	shredded Monterey Jack cheese	30 mL
	Nonstick cooking spray	
	Sour cream (optional)	
	Salsa (optional)	

1. In a small bowl, combine onion, green pepper, red pepper, cumin and salt.

2. Place both tortillas in bottom ring of sandwich maker. Top with chicken and cheese.

3. Lower cooking plate and top ring. Spray cooking plate with cooking spray. Add onion mixture to top ring.

4. Gently close the cover and cook for 4 to 5 minutes or until onion mixture is cooked to your liking (be careful not to overcook the tortillas). Rotate cooking plate away from sandwich maker and lift rings. Use a plastic or nylon spatula to remove the fajita.

5. If desired, top the fajita with sour cream and salsa. Serve immediately.

Anytime Bacon Quesadilla

For breakfast, lunch, dinner or a late-night snack, this quesadilla is the perfect Tex-Mex fix.

PREP TIME:
5 MINUTES

COOK TIME:
4 TO 5 MINUTES

Tips

If you prefer your onion and pepper more well done, sauté them first in melted butter or vegetable oil in a small skillet for about 3 minutes, or until soft and translucent.

If you cannot find 4-inch (10 cm) tortillas, cut larger ones down to size using a cookie cutter, kitchen scissors or the top of a wide-mouth canning jar ring.

♦ Preheat breakfast sandwich maker

1	large egg	1
1 tbsp	chopped onion	15 mL
1 tbsp	chopped green bell pepper	15 mL
Pinch	ground cumin	Pinch
Pinch	salt	Pinch
2	4-inch (10 cm) flour tortillas	2
2	slices bacon, cooked crisp and crumbled	2
2 tbsp	shredded Monterey Jack cheese	30 mL
	Nonstick cooking spray	
	Sour cream (optional)	
	Salsa (optional)	

1. In a small bowl, gently whisk egg. Stir in onion, green pepper, cumin and salt. Set aside.

2. Place one tortilla in bottom ring of sandwich maker. Top with bacon and cheese.

3. Lower the cooking plate and top ring. Lightly spray the plate with cooking spray, then pour in the egg mixture. Place the other tortilla on top of the egg.

4. Gently close the cover and cook for 4 to 5 minutes or until egg is cooked to your liking. Rotate cooking plate away from sandwich maker and lift rings. Use a plastic or nylon spatula to remove the quesadilla.

5. If desired, top the quesadilla with sour cream and salsa. Serve immediately.

Variation

For extra flavor and texture, add some sliced black olives with the bacon.

Pepperoni and Black Olive Pizza

While all pizzas have their roots in Italy, this mini version practically sings with Italian flavors. And it's so quick and easy, it makes a perfect afternoon snack or late-night treat.

PREP TIME:

3 MINUTES

COOK TIME:

3 TO 4 MINUTES

Tips

Look for small ready-made pizza crusts and pizza sauce in the Italian or deli section of your grocery store. The crusts come in multiples, often in a resealable bag, so you'll have more on hand for your pizza cravings.

If you are not able to find small pizza crusts, cut a larger crust into a 4-inch (10 cm) round using a cookie cutter, kitchen scissors or the top of a wide-mouth canning jar ring.

♦ Preheat breakfast sandwich maker

1	4-inch (10 cm) ready-made pizza crust (see tips, at left)	1
2 tbsp	pizza sauce	30 mL
2 tbsp	shredded mozzarella cheese	30 mL
1 tbsp	sliced black olives	15 mL
5	slices small pepperoni	5
1 tbsp	freshly grated Parmesan cheese (optional)	15 mL

1. Place crust in bottom ring of sandwich maker. Spread pizza sauce over crust. Sprinkle with mozzarella and olives. Arrange pepperoni on top.

2. Lower the cooking plate and top ring. Close the cover and cook for 3 to 4 minutes or until mozzarella is melted and crust edges are brown. Rotate cooking plate away from sandwich maker and lift rings. Use a plastic or nylon spatula to remove the pizza.

3. Let stand for 1 minute to allow mozzarella to set. Sprinkle with Parmesan, if desired. Serve immediately.

Kid-Friendly Options

◇◇

Peanut Butter, Banana and Chocolate Chip Sandwich

My childhood friend frequently had bananas in his peanut butter sandwich for lunch. I thought this was strange until I tried it myself. Many kids will agree that this tasty pairing, served warm with a bit of chocolate, makes an awesome sandwich.

PREP TIME:
3 MINUTES

COOK TIME:
4 TO 5 MINUTES

Tips

This sandwich is a great choice any time your kid gets hunger pangs.

Almond butter is a nice alternative to peanut butter in this recipe. The nutrients are very similar, but the almond butter has almost four times more calcium for growing bones.

♦ Preheat breakfast sandwich maker

2 tbsp	peanut butter	30 mL
2	slices whole wheat bread, cut into 4-inch (10 cm) rounds	2
1/3	banana, sliced	1/3
1 tbsp	mini chocolate chips	15 mL
	Nonstick cooking spray	

1. Spread peanut butter on one side of one bread slice. Place bread slice, spread side up, in bottom ring of sandwich maker. Top with banana and sprinkle with chocolate chips.

2. Lightly spray the underside of the cooking plate. Gently lower the cooking plate and top ring. Place the other bread slice in the top ring.

3. Gently close the cover and cook for 4 to 5 minutes or until sandwich is warmed through. Rotate cooking plate away from sandwich maker and lift rings. Use a plastic or nylon spatula to remove the sandwich. Serve immediately.

PB&J, Banana and Egg Sandwich

Most kids love peanut butter and jelly. When you add them to a breakfast sandwich, you get warm, gooey deliciousness.

PREP TIME:

3 MINUTES

COOK TIME:

4 TO 5 MINUTES

Tips

Because you cut the bread into rounds, it no longer has any crust — something most kids will be thankful for!

Cut the bread into 4-inch (10 cm) rounds using a cookie cutter, kitchen scissors or the top of a wide-mouth canning jar ring.

• Preheat breakfast sandwich maker

2 tbsp	peanut butter	30 mL
2 tsp	grape jelly	10 mL
2	slices whole wheat bread, cut into 4-inch (10 cm) rounds	2
3	thin slices banana	3
	Nonstick cooking spray	
1	large egg	1

1. Spread peanut butter and jelly on one side of each bread slice. Place one slice, spread side up, in bottom ring of sandwich maker. Top with banana.

2. Lower the cooking plate and top ring. Lightly spray the plate with cooking spray, then crack the egg into the ring. Pierce top of egg yolk with a toothpick or plastic fork. Place the other bread slice, spread side down, on top of the egg.

3. Gently close the cover and cook for 4 to 5 minutes or until egg is cooked to your liking. Rotate cooking plate away from sandwich maker and lift rings. Use a plastic or nylon spatula to remove the sandwich. Serve immediately.

Variation

Any type of jelly or jam will work in this sandwich, so pick your child's favorite.

Apple and Cheddar on Cinnamon Raisin Bread

The smell of toasted cinnamon raisin bread is a wonderful eye-opener in the morning. Combine it with melted Cheddar, apple slices and a fried egg, and kids and adults alike will be anxious to get out of bed.

PREP TIME:

3 MINUTES

COOK TIME:

4 TO 5 MINUTES

Tips

Ever wonder what to do with all those apples your kids get during their fall field trips to the apple farms? This sandwich is one nice option, and the kids will enjoy seeing their harvest added to their sandwiches.

Fuji, Honeycrisp and Gala apples are some of my favorites to use in this recipe. They are all sweet-tart and are a little crisper than others, giving this sandwich a nice crunch.

◆ Preheat breakfast sandwich maker

2	slices cinnamon raisin bread, cut into 4-inch (10 cm) rounds	2
1	slice Cheddar cheese	1
¼	apple, thinly sliced	¼
	Nonstick cooking spray	
1	large egg	1

1. Place one bread slice in bottom ring of sandwich maker. Top with cheese and apple.

2. Lower the cooking plate and top ring. Lightly spray the plate with cooking spray, then crack the egg into the ring. Pierce top of egg yolk with a toothpick or plastic fork. Place the other bread slice on top of the egg.

3. Gently close the cover and cook for 4 to 5 minutes or until egg is cooked to your liking. Rotate cooking plate away from sandwich maker and lift rings. Use a plastic or nylon spatula to remove the sandwich. Serve immediately.

Double Cheese and Egg White Sandwich

A grilled cheese sandwich is a welcome treat at any time of day. Serve with a warm cup of creamy tomato soup for the perfect meal.

PREP TIME:
2 MINUTES

COOK TIME:
3 TO 4 MINUTES

Tip

This sandwich gets a little slippery, with the egg white added on top of all the cheese, so be careful when removing it from the sandwich maker and while eating it. It is worth it!

- Preheat breakfast sandwich maker

2	slices whole wheat bread, cut into 4-inch (10 cm) rounds	2
2	slices Monterey Jack cheese	2
1	slice Cheddar cheese	1
	Nonstick cooking spray	
1	large egg white	1

1. Place one bread slice in bottom ring of sandwich maker. Top with Monterey Jack and Cheddar.

2. Lower the cooking plate and top ring. Lightly spray the plate with cooking spray, then add the egg white. Place the other bread slice on top of the egg.

3. Gently close the cover and cook for 3 to 4 minutes or until egg white is cooked through and no longer translucent. Rotate cooking plate away from sandwich maker and lift rings. Use a plastic or nylon spatula to remove the sandwich. Serve immediately.

Cream Cheese, Jam and Banana on Pancakes

Kids will almost think they are eating a banana split for breakfast or a snack with this tasty combination of strawberry jam, banana and cream cheese.

PREP TIME:
2 MINUTES

COOK TIME:
4 TO 5 MINUTES

Tip

What's a banana split without the whipped cream and maraschino cherry? Top this sandwich with a little whipped cream and a cherry, and you will be a real hit!

• Preheat breakfast sandwich maker

2 tsp	spreadable cream cheese	10 mL
2 tsp	strawberry jam	10 mL
2	frozen pancakes	2
1/3	banana, sliced	1/3
	Nonstick cooking spray	
1	large egg	1

1. Spread cream cheese and strawberry jam on one side of one pancake. Place pancake, spread side up, in bottom ring of sandwich maker. Top with banana.

2. Lower the cooking plate and top ring. Lightly spray the plate with cooking spray, then crack the egg into the ring. Pierce top of egg yolk with a toothpick or plastic fork. Place the other pancake on top of the egg.

3. Gently close the cover and cook for 4 to 5 minutes or until egg is cooked to your liking. Rotate cooking plate away from sandwich maker and lift rings. Use a plastic or nylon spatula to remove the sandwich. Serve immediately.

Variation

For a different flavor and a bit of crunch, use crunchy peanut butter instead of the cream cheese.

Caramel Apple Pancake Sandwich

Sometimes we just crave a caramel apple. This sandwich will help satisfy that craving.

Tips

A tart green apple, such as Granny Smith or Fuji, will make for a true caramel apple experience.

Serve the remainder of the apple alongside your sandwich or pack it in an airtight container for a midday snack.

* Preheat breakfast sandwich maker

¼	apple, chopped	¼
1 tbsp	packed brown sugar	15 mL
1 tbsp	butter, melted	15 mL
2	frozen pancakes	2
	Nonstick cooking spray	
1	large egg	1

1. In a small bowl, combine apple, brown sugar and butter.

2. Place one pancake in bottom ring of sandwich maker. Top with apple mixture.

3. Lower the cooking plate and top ring. Lightly spray the plate with cooking spray, then crack the egg into the ring. Pierce top of egg yolk with a toothpick or plastic fork. Place the other pancake on top of the egg.

4. Gently close the cover and cook for 4 to 5 minutes or until egg is cooked to your liking. Rotate cooking plate away from sandwich maker and lift rings. Use a plastic or nylon spatula to remove the sandwich. Serve immediately.

Variations

The apples can be tossed with 1 tbsp (15 mL) caramel syrup instead of the melted butter and brown sugar combination. If you make ice cream sundaes at home, you may already have caramel syrup on hand.

If you like your caramel apples dipped in nuts, sprinkle some chopped nuts on top of the apple mixture at the end of step 2.

Chocolate Chips, Egg and Cheese on Blueberry Pancakes

A touch of chocolate in a grab-and-go pancake sandwich is a great way to encourage your kids to eat breakfast.

PREP TIME:
2 MINUTES

COOK TIME:
4 TO 5 MINUTES

Tip

Kids will love the consistency of the softened mini chocolate chips, but chocolate syrup will also work. Only add up to 2 tsp (10 mL), so you don't lose the chocolate syrup in the bottom of the sandwich maker.

◆ Preheat breakfast sandwich maker

2	frozen blueberry pancakes	2
1	slice Colby cheese	1
1 tbsp	mini chocolate chips	15 mL
	Nonstick cooking spray	
1	large egg	1

1. Place one pancake in bottom ring of sandwich maker. Top with cheese and sprinkle with chocolate chips.

2. Lower the cooking plate and top ring. Lightly spray the plate with cooking spray, then crack the egg into the ring. Pierce top of egg yolk with a toothpick or plastic fork. Place the other pancake on top of the egg.

3. Gently close the cover and cook for 4 to 5 minutes or until egg is cooked to your liking. Rotate cooking plate away from sandwich maker and lift rings. Use a plastic or nylon spatula to remove the sandwich. Serve immediately.

Waffle S'mores

When you don't have a campfire going, the next best way to get the taste of s'mores is to use your breakfast sandwich maker!

PREP TIME:

2 MINUTES

COOK TIME:

3 TO 4 MINUTES

Tips

You can use square or triangular waffles if you cut them into circles to fit the sandwich maker. Use a round cookie cutter or kitchen shears to cut your waffles.

Lightly toast the waffles ahead of time for a crispier sandwich.

• Preheat breakfast sandwich maker

1 tbsp	chocolate hazelnut spread	15 mL
2 tbsp	marshmallow crème	30 mL
2	frozen round waffles	2
	Nonstick cooking spray	
1	large egg white	1

1. Spread chocolate hazelnut spread and marshmallow crème on one side of one waffle. Place waffle, spread side up, in bottom ring of sandwich maker.

2. Lightly spray the underside of the cooking plate with cooking spray. Lower the cooking plate and top ring. Lightly spray the top of the plate with cooking spray, then add the egg white. Place the other waffle on top of the egg white.

3. Gently close the cover and cook for 3 to 4 minutes or until egg white is cooked through and no longer translucent. Rotate cooking plate away from sandwich maker and lift rings. Use a plastic or nylon spatula to remove the sandwich. Serve immediately.

Variation

Instead of the chocolate hazelnut spread, drizzle 1 tbsp (15 mL) chocolate syrup into the holes of the bottom waffle, then spread the marshmallow crème on top.

Chicken Patty Sandwich

Now you can make this fast-food favorite at home, with your choice of toppings.

Tips

You can use a breaded or unbreaded chicken patty in this sandwich.

You can add frozen chicken patties directly to the breakfast sandwich maker, but if you find that they are not heating through in the specified time, try microwaving them on High for 30 to 60 seconds before adding them to the sandwich maker.

◆ Preheat breakfast sandwich maker

2 tsp	mayonnaise	10 mL
1	4-inch (10 cm) sandwich bun, split in half	1
	Lettuce (optional)	
1	slice tomato (optional)	1
2½ oz	frozen cooked chicken breast patty	75 g
	Nonstick cooking spray	
1	large egg	1

1. Spread mayonnaise on split side of top half of bun. Set aside.

2. Place bottom half of bun in bottom ring of sandwich maker. If desired, top with lettuce and tomato. Top with chicken patty.

3. Lower the cooking plate and top ring. Lightly spray the plate with cooking spray, then crack the egg into the ring. Pierce top of egg yolk with a toothpick or plastic fork. Place the other bun half, spread side down, on top of the egg.

4. Gently close the cover and cook for 4 to 5 minutes or until an instant-read thermometer inserted in the center of the chicken patty registers 165°F (74°C). Rotate cooking plate away from sandwich maker and lift rings. Use a plastic or nylon spatula to remove the sandwich. Serve immediately.

Chicken Quesadilla

Quesadillas are a great appetizer or snack. Your kids will keep asking for this Mexican-style treat.

PREP TIME:

3 MINUTES

COOK TIME:

3 TO 4 MINUTES

Tips

Cut the finished quesadilla into little triangles for your child to dip in salsa, guacamole or sour cream.

The salad bar at your grocery store likely offers all of the ingredients you need to fill these quesadillas, as well as sliced black olives, red and green bell peppers, onions and a host of other favorite quesadilla fillings. You can pick up just what you need for as few or as many quesadillas as you like.

♦ Preheat breakfast sandwich maker

2	4-inch (10 cm) flour tortillas	2
2 tbsp	chopped roasted chicken	30 mL
2 tbsp	shredded Colby cheese	30 mL
1 tbsp	salsa	15 mL
	Nonstick cooking spray	
1	large egg white	1

1. Place one tortilla in bottom ring of sandwich maker. Top with chicken, cheese and salsa.

2. Lower the cooking plate and top ring. Lightly spray the plate with cooking spray, then add the egg white. Place the other tortilla on top of the egg.

3. Gently close the cover and cook for 3 to 4 minutes or until egg white is cooked through and no longer translucent. Rotate cooking plate away from sandwich maker and lift rings. Use a plastic or nylon spatula to remove the quesadilla. Serve immediately.

Pepperoni Pizza

It's a rare kid who doesn't love pizza, and this mini version makes a quick and easy snack. Make sure you have ingredients for more than one serving ready to go, because once this pizza comes out of the sandwich maker, everyone will be clamoring for more!

PREP TIME:

3 MINUTES

COOK TIME:

3 TO 4 MINUTES

Tip

Purchase small pepperoni slices in 7-oz (200 g) bags, which hold almost 100 slices. They last well in the refrigerator (and barely take up any room!), so it's easy to keep them on hand for quick pizzas.

• Preheat breakfast sandwich maker

1	4-inch (10 cm) ready-made pizza crust (see tips, page 159)	1
2 tbsp	pizza sauce	30 mL
2 tbsp	shredded mozzarella cheese	30 mL
5	slices small pepperoni	5
1 tbsp	freshly grated Parmesan cheese (optional)	15 mL

1. Place crust in bottom ring of sandwich maker. Spread pizza sauce over crust. Sprinkle with mozzarella. Arrange pepperoni on top.

2. Lower the cooking plate and top ring. Close the cover and cook for 3 to 4 minutes or until mozzarella is melted and crust edges are brown. Rotate cooking plate away from sandwich maker and lift rings. Use a plastic or nylon spatula to remove the pizza.

3. Let stand for 1 minute to allow mozzarella to set. Sprinkle with Parmesan, if desired. Serve immediately.

Ham and Pineapple Pizza

Pineapple and ham add sweetness and tropical flair to this mini pizza.

PREP TIME:
4 MINUTES

COOK TIME:
3 TO 4 MINUTES

Tip

If your pizza gets to be piled high with toppings, and you don't want them touching the bottom of the cooking plate, you can rotate the plate away from the sandwich maker before lowering the top ring. The plate will be very hot, so be very careful when handling it and when lowering the ring, and be careful not to touch the plate at any time during the cooking process. Make sure to keep your kids well away while the pizza is cooking.

♦ Preheat breakfast sandwich maker

1	4-inch (10 cm) ready-made pizza crust (see tips, page 159)	1
2 tbsp	pizza sauce	30 mL
2 tbsp	shredded mozzarella cheese, divided	30 mL
2 tbsp	finely chopped cooked ham	30 mL
1 tbsp	drained canned or fresh pineapple tidbits	15 mL
Pinch	hot pepper flakes (optional)	Pinch
1 tbsp	freshly grated Parmesan cheese (optional)	15 mL

1. Place crust in bottom ring of sandwich maker. Spread pizza sauce over crust. Sprinkle with half of the mozzarella. Arrange ham and pineapple on top, then sprinkle with the remaining mozzarella.

2. Lower the cooking plate and top ring. Close the cover and cook for 3 to 4 minutes or until mozzarella is melted and crust edges are brown. Rotate cooking plate away from sandwich maker and lift rings. Use a plastic or nylon spatula to remove the pizza.

3. Let stand for 1 minute to allow mozzarella to set. Sprinkle with hot pepper flakes and Parmesan, if desired. Serve immediately.

Variation

For golden, caramelized grilled pineapple, use pineapple chunks or a pineapple ring. Instead of adding the pineapple in step 1, spray the cooking plate with nonstick cooking spray and add the pineapple to the plate.

Desserts and Snacks

◇◇

Berry Granola Parfait on Pancakes

Creamy, delicate ricotta cheese, berries and granola combine for a sweet and crunchy dessert.

PREP TIME:
2 MINUTES

COOK TIME:
3 TO 4 MINUTES

Tips

You can use a few fresh raspberries instead of the raspberry jam; add them with the granola in step 1.

Any combination of small berries will work well in and/ or on this sandwich. Just be careful not to overpack the sandwich with berries.

◆ Preheat breakfast sandwich maker

1 tbsp	raspberry jam	15 mL
1 tbsp	ricotta cheese	15 mL
2	frozen pancakes	2
1½ tbsp	granola, divided	22 mL
	Nonstick cooking spray	
1	large egg white	1
	Yogurt	
	Strawberries and/or blueberries	

1. Spread raspberry jam and ricotta on one side of one pancake. Place pancake, spread side up, in bottom ring of sandwich maker. Sprinkle with 1 tbsp (15 mL) granola.

2. Lower the cooking plate and top ring. Lightly spray the plate with cooking spray, then add the egg white. Place the other pancake on top of the egg.

3. Gently close the cover and cook for 3 to 4 minutes or until egg white is cooked through and no longer translucent. Rotate cooking plate away from sandwich maker and lift rings. Use a plastic or nylon spatula to remove the sandwich.

4. Serve immediately, topped with a dollop of yogurt, berries and the remaining granola.

Peanut Butter, Banana and Granola Sandwich

This protein-packed power sandwich is great when you need an extra boost of energy.

PREP TIME:
2 MINUTES

COOK TIME:
4 TO 5 MINUTES

Tips

If your bananas are very ripe, mash them and spread them on the bottom slice of bread, on top of the peanut butter.

You can omit the egg from this sandwich. If you do, rotate the cooking plate away from the sandwich maker before adding the top bread slice. The plate will be very hot, so be very careful when handling it and when lowering the ring, and be careful not to touch the plate at any time during the cooking process.

◆ Preheat breakfast sandwich maker

2 tbsp	peanut butter	30 mL
2	slices whole wheat bread, cut into 4-inch (20 cm) rounds	2
1 tbsp	granola	15 mL
3	slices banana	3
	Nonstick cooking spray	
1	large egg	1

1. Spread peanut butter on one side of each bread slice. Place one slice, spread side up, in bottom ring of sandwich maker. Sprinkle with granola. Top with banana.

2. Lower the cooking plate and top ring. Lightly spray the plate with cooking spray, then crack the egg into the ring. Pierce top of egg yolk with a toothpick or plastic fork. Place the other bread slice, spread side down, on top of the egg.

3. Gently close the cover and cook for 4 to 5 minutes or until egg is cooked to your liking. Rotate cooking plate away from sandwich maker and lift rings. Use a plastic or nylon spatula to remove the sandwich. Serve immediately.

Pumpkin and Spice Sandwich

Pumpkin pie is a favorite fall and holiday dessert. Now you can enjoy the same flavor in a rich-tasting sandwich.

PREP TIME:
2 MINUTES

COOK TIME:
4 TO 5 MINUTES

Tip

I love baking fresh cooking pumpkins. If you do too, save a little extra pumpkin for this recipe. Here's an easy way to bake a fresh pumpkin: Cut it in half, remove the seeds and place it cut side down on a rimmed baking sheet. Bake in a preheated 350°F (180°C) oven for about 1 hour or until the pumpkin starts to caramelize and the skin depresses easily when touched.

◆ Preheat breakfast sandwich maker

1	crusty roll, split in half	1
1 tsp	spreadable cream cheese	5 mL
3 tbsp	pumpkin purée (not pie filling)	45 mL
Pinch	ground cinnamon	Pinch
Pinch	ground nutmeg	Pinch
Pinch	ground ginger	Pinch
	Nonstick cooking spray	
1	large egg	1

1. Scoop out a little of the softer bread in the middle of the bottom half of the roll. Spread cream cheese on scooped side of roll half. Place roll half, spread side up, in bottom ring of sandwich maker. Add pumpkin, 1 tbsp (15 mL) at a time, smoothing it over the roll. Sprinkle with cinnamon, nutmeg and ginger.

2. Lower the cooking plate and top ring. Lightly spray the plate with cooking spray, then crack the egg into the ring. Pierce top of egg yolk with a toothpick or plastic fork. Place the other roll half, split side down, on top of the egg.

3. Gently close the cover and cook for 4 to 5 minutes or until egg is cooked to your liking. Rotate cooking plate away from sandwich maker and lift rings. Use a plastic or nylon spatula to remove the sandwich. Serve immediately.

Pear, Blue Cheese and Pecan Sandwich

The combination of blue cheese, pears and pecans makes for a wonderful light snack.

PREP TIME:
9 TO 10 MINUTES

COOK TIME:
4 TO 5 MINUTES

Tips

To toast chopped nuts, place them in a metal pie plate or cake pan and toast in a preheated 350°F (180°C) oven for 3 minutes. Gently shake the pan to redistribute the nuts. Continue toasting for 3 to 4 minutes, or until nuts are golden brown and fragrant.

Instead of a fresh pear, you can use pears from a 4-oz (113 mL) snack container or small can. Use half the container for your sandwich and serve the remainder on the side. Peaches and apples also work nicely in this sandwich, and also come in ready-to-eat fruit cups.

◆ Preheat breakfast sandwich maker

1	English muffin, split in half	1
2 tbsp	crumbled blue cheese	30 mL
1/4	pear, sliced	1/4
1 tbsp	toasted chopped pecans	15 mL
	Nonstick cooking spray	
1	large egg	1

1. Place one English muffin half, split side up, in bottom ring of sandwich maker. Top with blue cheese, pear and pecans.

2. Lower the cooking plate and top ring. Lightly spray the plate with cooking spray, then crack the egg into the ring. Pierce top of egg yolk with a toothpick or plastic fork. Place the other muffin half on top of the egg.

3. Gently close the cover and cook for 4 to 5 minutes or until egg is cooked to your liking. Rotate cooking plate away from sandwich maker and lift rings. Use a plastic or nylon spatula to remove the sandwich. Serve immediately.

Cream Cheese and Jam on Challah

If you serve this dreamy warm sandwich as an after-school treat, be forewarned that every kid on the block may start popping in.

PREP TIME:
2 MINUTES

COOK TIME:
3 TO 4 MINUTES

Tip

For the ultimate decadent afternoon treat, serve with a side of warm chocolate syrup for dipping.

• Preheat breakfast sandwich maker

2 tbsp	spreadable cream cheese	30 mL
2 tbsp	strawberry jam	30 mL
2	slices challah bread, cut into 4-inch (20 cm) rounds	2
	Nonstick cooking spray	
1	large egg white	1
	Confectioners' (icing) sugar (optional)	

1. Spread cream cheese and strawberry jam over one side of each bread slice. Place one slice, spread side up, in bottom ring of sandwich maker.

2. Lower the cooking plate and top ring. Lightly spray the plate with cooking spray, then add the egg white. Place the other bread slice, spread side down, on top of the egg white.

3. Gently close the cover and cook for 3 to 4 minutes or until egg white is cooked through and no longer translucent. Rotate cooking plate away from sandwich maker and lift rings. Use a plastic or nylon spatula to remove the sandwich.

4. Sprinkle sandwich with confectioners' sugar, if desired. Serve immediately.

Variations

Use any of your favorite jams in place of the strawberry jam.

Challah bread gives this sandwich a sweet flavor, but whole wheat, sourdough or white bread will also work well.

Caramel Sundae Sandwich

The sweet, gooey goodness of melted caramel, cream cheese and walnuts will remind you of an ice cream sandwich.

PREP TIME:
2 MINUTES

COOK TIME:
4 TO 5 MINUTES

Tips

Cut the sandwich into little triangles and serve with a side of warm caramel or chocolate sauce for dipping.

You may want to press the cream cheese down in the center of the flatbread as you are spreading it, making a little indent. This will help prevent the caramel sauce from running out of the sides of the sandwich.

◆ Preheat breakfast sandwich maker

2 tbsp	spreadable cream cheese	30 mL
2	slices flatbread, cut into 4-inch (20 cm) rounds	2 2
1 tbsp	finely chopped walnuts	15 mL
1 tbsp	caramel sauce	15 mL
	Nonstick cooking spray	
1	large egg	1

1. Spread cream cheese on one side of one flatbread slice. Place flatbread, spread side up, in bottom ring of sandwich maker. Sprinkle with walnuts and drizzle with caramel sauce.

2. Lower the cooking plate and top ring. Lightly spray the plate with cooking spray, then crack the egg into the ring. Pierce top of egg yolk with a toothpick or plastic fork. Place the other flatbread slice on top of the egg.

3. Gently close the cover and cook for 4 to 5 minutes or until egg is cooked to your liking. Rotate cooking plate away from sandwich maker and lift rings. Use a plastic or nylon spatula to remove the sandwich. Serve immediately.

Strawberry Rhubarb Shortcake

Sweet strawberries and tart rhubarb combine with rich and creamy mascarpone for a dessert that will remind you of strawberry cheesecake.

PREP TIME:

2 MINUTES

COOK TIME:

3 TO 4 MINUTES

Tip

If you don't have honey butter, you can make your own by mixing 1 tsp (5 mL) liquid honey with 1 tsp (5 mL) softened butter.

Sprinkle with a little confectioners' (icing) sugar and top with sliced fresh strawberries. Serve with a scoop of ice cream on the side.

◆ Preheat breakfast sandwich maker

2 tsp	honey butter (see tip, at left), softened	10 mL
2	slices shortcake, cut into 4-inch (20 cm) rounds	2
2 tbsp	mascarpone cheese	30 mL
2 tbsp	strawberry rhubarb preserves	30 mL

1. Spread honey butter on one side of each shortcake slice. Spread mascarpone and preserves on top of honey butter on bottom shortcake slice. Carefully place bottom shortcake slice, spread side up, in bottom ring of sandwich maker.

2. Lower the cooking plate and top ring. Place the other shortcake slice, spread side down, on plate.

3. Gently close the cover and cook for 3 to 4 minutes or until shortbread is toasted and sandwich is warmed through. Rotate cooking plate away from sandwich maker and lift rings. Use a plastic or nylon spatula to remove the sandwich. Serve immediately.

Marmalade, White Chocolate and Coconut Sandwich

Orange marmalade, white chocolate chips and shredded coconut combine wonderfully in this sweet and slightly chewy sandwich, for a delicious treat.

PREP TIME:
2 MINUTES

COOK TIME:
4 TO 5 MINUTES

Tips

Either sweetened or unsweetened coconut will work well in this recipe.

For added crunch, sprinkle some chia seeds or chopped nuts on top of the egg.

♦ Preheat breakfast sandwich maker

2 tbsp	orange marmalade	30 mL
1	English muffin, split in half	1
1 tbsp	white chocolate chips	15 mL
2 tbsp	packed shredded coconut	30 mL
	Nonstick cooking spray	
1	large egg	1

1. Spread marmalade on split sides of English muffin. Place one muffin half, spread side up, in bottom ring of sandwich maker. Sprinkle with white chocolate chips and coconut.

2. Lower the cooking plate and top ring. Lightly spray the plate with cooking spray, then crack the egg into the ring. Pierce top of egg yolk with a toothpick or plastic fork. Place the other muffin half, spread side down, on top of the egg.

3. Gently close the cover and cook for 4 to 5 minutes or until egg is cooked to your liking. Rotate cooking plate away from sandwich maker and lift rings. Use a plastic or nylon spatula to remove the sandwich. Serve immediately.

Baklava-Inspired Biscuit

Baklava is a rich dessert made with layers and layers of buttered phyllo pastry. It is wonderfully sweet, but is challenging to make. This sandwich, made with a buttery, flaky biscuit, is a fast and delicious alternative.

PREP TIME:
3 MINUTES

COOK TIME:
4 TO 5 MINUTES

Tips

This sandwich is quite sweet, so you may want to split it in half and share it.

* Preheat breakfast sandwich maker

1	large egg	1
Dash	vanilla extract	Dash
2 tsp	butter, melted	10 mL
1	baking powder biscuit, split in half	1
1 tsp	liquid honey	5 mL
1 tbsp	chopped walnuts	15 mL
Pinch	ground cinnamon	Pinch
	Nonstick cooking spray	

1. In a small bowl, gently whisk together egg and vanilla. Set aside.

2. Brush butter on split sides of biscuit. Place one biscuit half, butter side up, in bottom ring of sandwich maker. Drizzle with honey and sprinkle with walnuts and cinnamon.

3. Lower the cooking plate and top ring. Lightly spray the plate with cooking spray, then pour in the egg mixture. Place the other biscuit, butter side down, on top of the egg.

4. Gently close the cover and cook for 4 to 5 minutes or until egg is cooked to your liking. Rotate cooking plate away from sandwich maker and lift rings. Use a plastic or nylon spatula to remove the sandwich. Serve immediately.

Variations

Chopped hazelnuts, chopped pistachios or sliced almonds are also often used in baklava and can be substituted for the walnuts here.

Toffee, Honey and Pecan Biscuit

This sweet, crunchy sandwich tastes like your own homemade candy bar.

PREP TIME:

2 MINUTES

COOK TIME:

3 TO 4 MINUTES

Tip

If you cannot find toffee baking bits, you can break a toffee candy bar into small pieces. The candy bars are typically coated in chocolate, which is a fun addition to this sandwich treat.

• Preheat breakfast sandwich maker

2 tsp	liquid honey	10 mL
1	baking powder biscuit, split in half	1
1½ tbsp	toffee baking bits	22 mL
1 tbsp	sliced pecans	15 mL
	Nonstick cooking spray	
1	large egg white	1
Pinch	ground cinnamon	Pinch

1. Drizzle honey over split sides of biscuit. Place one biscuit half, honey side up, in bottom ring of sandwich maker. Sprinkle with toffee bits and pecans.

2. Lower the cooking plate and top ring. Lightly spray the plate with cooking spray, then add the egg white. Sprinkle with cinnamon. Place the other biscuit, honey side down, on top of the egg.

3. Gently close the cover and cook for 3 to 4 minutes or until egg white is cooked through and no longer translucent. Rotate cooking plate away from sandwich maker and lift rings. Use a plastic or nylon spatula to remove the sandwich. Serve immediately.

Variation

To make this sandwich taste even more like a candy bar, replace the biscuit with two 4-inch (10 cm) flour tortillas. Leave a bit of space between the drizzled honey and the edge of the tortillas so the honey does not flow out the sides.

Sausage and Green Olive Pizza

This mini pizza is easy to make, perfect for an afternoon snack or a late-night treat.

Tips

Look for small ready-made pizza crusts and pizza sauce in the Italian or deli section of your grocery store. The crusts come in multiples, often in a resealable bag, so you'll have more on hand for your pizza cravings.

If you are not able to find small pizza crusts, cut a larger crust into a 4-inch (10 cm) round using a cookie cutter, kitchen scissors or the top of a wide-mouth canning jar ring.

• Preheat breakfast sandwich maker

1	4-inch (10 cm) ready-made pizza crust (see tips, at left)	1
2 tbsp	pizza sauce	30 mL
2 tbsp	shredded mozzarella cheese	30 mL
1 tbsp	sliced green olives	15 mL
2 tbsp	cooked bulk Italian sausage	30 mL
1 tsp	olive oil	5 mL
2 tsp	chopped red onion	10 mL
1 tbsp	freshly grated Parmesan cheese (optional)	15 mL

1. Place crust in bottom ring of sandwich maker. Spread pizza sauce over crust. Sprinkle with mozzarella, olives and sausage.

2. Lower the cooking plate and top ring. Add oil and red onion to the plate. Close the cover and cook for 3 to 4 minutes or until mozzarella is melted and crust edges are brown. Rotate cooking plate away from sandwich maker and lift rings. Use a plastic or nylon spatula to remove the pizza.

3. Let stand for 1 minute to allow mozzarella to set. Sprinkle with Parmesan, if desired. Serve immediately.

Index

Library and Archives Canada Cataloguing in Publication

Williams, Jennifer (Cookbook author)
   150 best breakfast sandwich maker recipes / Jennifer Williams.

Includes index.
ISBN 978-0-7788-0484-0 (pbk.)

   1. Breakfasts. 2. Sandwiches. 3. Cookbooks. I. Title.
II. Title: One hundred fifty best breakfast sandwich maker recipes.

TX733.W54 2014   641.5'2   C2014-903333-8